Contents

Prologue

There are many very sincere and thoughtful people who are salaried, sponsored or generously volunteering, endlessly going to and fro in the earth crying "Peace! Peace!"... But there is actually very little genuine peace in our world today. We have tens of thousands of aid workers and peace-keepers from many faithful nations, valiantly seeking to help bring law, order and civility into this troubled world. Sadly however, they often have little or no authority to act, few resources, conflicting objectives, and are therefore able to achieve very little, in the difficult situations in which they are placed.

There are also many examples of well-intended people who are seeking peace, both personally and corporately, using methods which are flawed in strategy or implementation and have little or no chance of success.

This book seeks to describe some of the various forms of peace which we all need and yearn for, highlighting some of the reasons why we fail or have difficulty in finding this place... and also suggests some strategic, multifaceted and practical approaches to achieving the genuine article.

Over the millennia, many have sought to bring solutions to these challenges, but few have succeeded. The process usually breaks down and becomes ineffective over time, or worse still is not viable from the very beginning.

I trust you will find this book helpful, enlightening and yet at the same time immensely simple, practical and effective in the treatment of this critically important subject.

Please enjoy!!!

David Apelt

Chapter 1 - The Search Begins

It was more than thirty years ago now, when I first seriously considered the issue of what peace really is. I was a happily married young man with a lovely wife, two precious daughters and a new baby son. Work was extremely busy, as was family life and we were also leaders of a steadily renewing suburban church which was seeking to rediscover what Jesus' gospel was meant to look like and how it should be lived and presented in our generation. We'd just had 'the recession that we had to have', which was engineered by the central bank, bringing government and ultimately community interest rates to a punitive and ridiculous level. This put many in our community into financial difficulty and some totally lost their livelihood for an extended period of time. As a community and nation, we were dealing with drugs, crime and various forms of corruption and abuse. There were ongoing theatres of war on various continents all of which seemed interminable and difficult to resolve. These were certainly not times of peace! Yet I seemed inexorably drawn to personally seek out and document this elusive topic in some level of practical detail. This journey was to take two years in all, and still continues to this day...

Have you ever found yourself in a place of pure, unadulterated Peace? That ethereal state of being so wonderfully at ease, that all of our troubles seem to fade away and we feel so relaxed, that the cares of our world just don't seem to matter anymore. Of course, all the issues are still there, but for the moment anyway, the burdens, fears, confusion and anxiety have all gone.

A noticeable result of being in this state is that one's mind begins to become more clear, relaxed, energized and focused. This then creates a feeling of having more time to reflect and a receptive state of readiness to listen and process our thoughts, while also setting a good foundation to encounter true refreshment, healing, recovery and increased potential.

This *genuine peace* is the mysterious phenomenon which this book seeks to explore, and to describe ways in which it can be achieved, more readily and more often, in our normal, complex and busy lives.

I'm sure you have on occasions at least, even if only partially, experienced this type of amazing feeling. It can be brought on by a favourite place, a positive soothing atmosphere, a wonderful memory or song, even a person you are with whose very presence and spirit can bring you to this place.

One thing I have observed though is that this idyllic state is not fully achievable without some assistance from outside of ourselves... and I've found that the source of that help is of critical importance as well!

This is due to the fact that seeking peace in all the wrong places can destroy a person, and any semblance of peace that is found in such places is always a counterfeit of the real thing and will exact a devastating price on the human spirit.

I have good friends who have searched their whole life for this particular type of peace. Often, we don't even know what we are looking for, but we know we are missing something important. There is a constant yearning inside our soul which creates an unsettled state of the heart, never being satisfied until we eventually find the real thing.

One particular friend, Angel, tried every different philosophy or modality she could lay her hands on, but she was never satisfied. Something was always amiss. The promise was never delivered. All the effort, discipline, dedication and passion she invested trying to master each new discipline failed to deliver on promise. Some led to dead ends with no results and no helpful answers.

Others deceptively drew her deeper into the maze, endlessly devouring her time on methods, processes, patterns, fasts, mantras, 'prayers' etc. And there was always the promise of discovering more 'secrets', 'special knowledge', 'euphoric states', 'miracle releases', 'supernatural power' and such. It was a never ending and distracting treadmill of fruitless activity.

After 35 years of endless and exhausting search, Angel finally encountered a young workmate, who shared with her regarding The Way... She immediately saw truth in what her friend was sharing with her and accepted the essence of this profound, yet simple life-changing narrative and world view. Then once again she committed herself to passionately explore this new way of life. Astoundingly as soon as she had made that conscious choice, she found her eyes were instantly opened to the truth of this good news. At last, she had finally found the path of *genuine peace*! She was never the same again. More on this later!

Finally, I should point out that this book is highly summarized in form and content and because of the broad nature of the subject, seeks to explore, at times in quite abbreviated fashion, a vast array of issues, concepts and principles, as well as personal accounts of individuals who have experienced such matters firsthand... I trust you will find this approach beneficial and productive.

Chapter 2 - Definition of *Genuine Peace*

The concept of *genuine peace*, which is at the heart of this book, is a combination of the Hebrew word *shalom*, the Greek word *eirene* and the English word peace, as well as any other words from which these three have been derived. *Genuine peace* includes such characteristics as:-

- Feeling safe, secure, settled and protected
- Having a sense of being provided for, nurtured, succoured and faring well
- Being debt-free, unencumbered
- Having no stress, worry, anxiety
- Being in good relationship with others
- Having a sense of hope, joy and happiness
- Having faith that all things will ultimately work together for good for you and yours
- Being blessed, favoured and preferred
- Being in good health and wellbeing in body, soul and spirit
- Having a sense of prospering, flourishing and succeeding
- Feeling that anything which has been lost will ultimately be restored
- That your borders are secure and vital places robust and intact
- A knowing that your internal resources are intact and in good supply
- And external supplies are abundantly available when needed

- Being certain that you can deliver on any reasonable assignment you are asked to accomplish
- Knowing that you can recover from any past problems which may have occurred
- That any loss can be made good
- That you have access to earthly and heavenly wisdom for life
- Having a healthy sense of giving and receiving
- Being complete, full, satisfied, whole, lacking nothing
- Able to maintain a place or attitude of solitude, quietness and rest in the midst of any challenge
- Being in a multifaceted State of ONE-ness
- One with God
- One with humankind
- One with self
- One with spouse
- One with family
- One with friends
- One with acquaintances
- One with workmates
- One with enemies
- One with the earth
- One with creatures
- One with plants
- One with the *'universe!'* as it were.

It means being totally and seriously at peace with God, with self and with any other good thing. I say 'good' because one should never seek to be at peace with evil. That is a sure way to lose our peace.

Now let's explore a couple of accounts from my own life which may help to further define this concept of *genuine peace*. When I reflect back over my life, I remember from the very beginning feeling a sense of settled peace in my heart. My very first recollections of being a person, and existing on this earth, which I suspect was when I was three or four years old, were always feelings of safety and being loved, appreciated, nurtured and provided for, even though I now know those were very difficult times for my Mum and Dad. I was always aware of God as well and knew that He was looking over me and my family in a positive, affirming and supportive way. This familiar yet beautiful and always greatly appreciated peace has remained with me my whole life. So I am therefore very aware when I lose that peace or it 'loses' me for some reason. If you've never experienced this peace, I can assure you that it is always there, available to be entered into. The journey toward this peace can often be circuitous and varied but I've become convinced it is there for the asking, to be had by all who will come and genuinely seek it out.

Thinking on this topic reminds me of a time a little over twenty years ago when I was experiencing some really serious health problems which were threatening my well-being and possibly even my life. I was covered head to toe with very serious eczema, struggling to find any food which I could eat which wouldn't make me feel uncomfortable in one way of another. My morale was flagging, and I was beginning to feel like a burden on my family, and struggling to fulfill all my responsibilities in life, work, family and church. These were difficult days indeed. One advantage of hardship though is that it often draws us closer to God. I began to read, reflect, pray, research, make enquiries and generally explore all the avenues I could think of, where possible answers may be found. Initially this was out of a state of steadily increasing anxiety, worry or even fear. Which I must say is one of the arch enemies of peace. But then something happened which helped me immensely. While I was going through this anxious journey I experienced on a number of occasions, some happenings that one might call cameos or interludes of *genuine peace*. This surprised me a little because I had not yet found any satisfactory answers and was still only just managing to cope with the onerous symptoms of this debilitating health condition.

One day while reflecting on the parlous state of my circumstances and wondering whether I was going to make it through intact, I had a memory of a place which I had first seen in my mind when I was in primary school. I wrote a small descriptive essay, sharing the ambience of this scene with my teacher and fellow classmates. As I drew this faint memory back into mind, the picture began to crystallize, becoming more clear and beautiful by the moment, then slowly began to evolve and extend in my mind's eye.

I was immediately aware of the presence of a *dear friend*, there with me. Close alongside, yet not within view. His presence made me feel safe and secure and I was beginning to feel peace, even though I had been and still was very troubled by my plight. I felt like I lacked nothing, even though I was still in the midst of difficulty and was quietly confident that everything would work out alright in the end. Then I felt gently compelled to lay down on the soft, cool, green, clover, growing alongside this most delightful babbling brook. I felt cool and comforted, itching of the skin subsided and I began to relax, slowed my breathing and took a couple of long deep breaths, resembling that of a soothing, satisfying sigh. The brook was glistening and chortling, trickling therapeutically amongst the rocks. On the one hand, clear, crisp and transparent like glass. On the other, there were randomly scattered, opaque, foaming bubbles, spasmodically obscuring the silver, black and brightly coloured fish which were meandering to and fro under the surface. The gentle, sparkling rhythms of the stream soothed and restored my soul. I just knew that there would be a pathway through my troubles. Even though I had brushed with the possibility of death on and off this last year, as I sought answers to my dilemmas, I was at last beginning to settle on the idea that I would recover, and fear of the unknown began to leave me. Then as I began to lift my eyes off the problems at hand, I noticed in the distance, through a narrow, dark, ominous cleft in the surrounding rocky cliff, a faint light, shining hopefully from the crevice. As I approach this place, I noticed that with thoughtful discipline one could walk through this gap in the rock toward that tantalizing light. This made me feel very hopeful and excited at the prospect of discovering some answers in that mesmerizing, compelling glow at the end of the tunnel. Once I' d worked my way deftly through the dark places, I realized I didn't have to fear the evil which may lurk there, because my dear friend was still with me. Then suddenly on reaching the end of that dark place, the vista opened up into a number of large green meadows and rolling hills, strewn with trees and shrubs, and an abundantly provisioned picnic table was placed right there on centre stage. I suddenly realized that everything would be alright, and that full provision had already been made to deal with whatever I was going to be facing in life. The anxiety and worry left me immediately and a wonderful, settled peace, which I was soon able to share with my family, slowly settled over me, in me, and through me. Even though those troubling feelings sometimes return, I am ever reminded of the provision that has already been made for us to enjoy this wonderful place of peace.

Are you getting a feel of how marvellous this *genuine peace* really is? If only we could fully achieve it in our lives here on earth! The good news is that this book will hopefully demonstrate satisfactorily that such peace is actually possible. Although never perfectly achieved in this life, it can be approached with a large degree of success, with the appropriate processes, methods, mindsets, values, relationships and worldview.

There is however, a strong prerequisite for this type of peace. Such amazing peace in all its fullness requires an appropriately worthy *peace offering*... a free-will, totally voluntary, pure, high value, sacrificial, intermediary act of mercy, in order to make it all possible.

And then there are the *Peacemakers*... Those world-changing dedicated miracle workers, who as well as working tirelessly on experiencing a good measure of this peace in their own lives, are also able to thoughtfully and effectively help other individuals to do so as well. I have learned and observed firsthand that we all have this innate potential to become peacemakers.

There is much more on these topics in later chapters, but before examining this wonderful peace in more detail, let's first look at some practical examples of the absence of this type of peace.

Chapter 3 - Absence of Peace

It was in the balmy European summer of nineteen ninety-six, that I found myself on a business mission with a senior colleague, exploring the future evolution and possibilities of information technology and communications (IT&C) in the five-to-ten-year strategic planning time horizon. My company was a large, international financial services organization seeking to chart an optimal way forward for its information technology and services platform. We sought to chart a path which took into account optimal considerations regarding availability, affordability, practical efficiency, viability and the like. It was a particularly difficult task in that these were the still early days in the discovery and development of integrated computer and communications systems and applications for financial services. Technology was advancing at a phenomenal rate, customers were demanding the latest trendy technology and the enormous pressures of competition were pressing in, particularly from smaller more 'agile' companies. The practical realities however, of the need for affordability, efficiency, effectiveness, speedy time to market and the need to make the customer experience as seamless as possible, all served to present us with impossible, conflicting objectives. It was always a fine balance between the risk of very costly mistakes versus criticisms from particularly non-technical business colleagues, who wanted everything at once, immediately, and did not understand the enormous cost, risks, development and systems integration endeavours, as well as the implications and complexity of change. These were difficult, indeed quite significantly stressful times. Yet turned out to be some of the most extremely satisfying learning places of my life... as well as the most frustrating, because of the often near impossibility of what we were being asked or indeed expected to do. One needed to be a miracle worker and have the prophetic insight, as well as practical engineering, conceptual and design abilities in order to effectively see into the future. We needed to observe what was coming, understand the needs of our customers, discern what was possible, make a call on which technologies and IT&C companies would succeed, and be viable, cost effective and practically achievable. It was a daunting yet equally satisfying task, one for which I had a very real sense of call, and an unexplainable confidence and peace that there were no unanswerable questions, that we would always be able to find a sensible way forward and be able to articulate this to our internal and external customers as required.

So here we were on the outskirts of breathtakingly beautiful London on a long weekend taking some time-out from an exhausting itinerary of fact finding and strategy development. We had been sight-seeing to as many traditional sites that we could fit in on Saturday and Sunday. My workmate was keen to show me the highlights. He'd been there before but some time back and I felt I may never have the privilege to come this way again, although as it turned out I was blessed to be able to return a few years later and explore those same sights with my dear first wife, June. Now the next day was usually a working day, but had been declared a public holiday, and my workmate had to go and see a family friend. So here I was on my own in one of the biggest cities in the world with one day free to explore, and lots of options. Initially I thought rest might be the best option but with further thought considered that would be a waste of a day in such an iconic location. So I chose a museum in the suburbs just outside of the central business district specializing in ancient history. Duly loaded up with research information, maps and snacks I tentatively ventured into the megalithic London rail system and boarded what was hopefully the correct train. Eventually, I arrived at the place where the museum was supposed to be somewhat weary from the journey, since this was my third day of touring. Then after walking thirty minutes or so on an uncomfortably warm humid morning I found the imposing Roman-looking building with a massive, long and ornate set of white marble stairs, slightly wet and very slippery, from recent rain. Well, you may have guessed. After two hours of travel in totally unfamiliar territory, and among the often scary-seeming characters one can encounter on a subway, I had arrived. Then... having walked for a further thirty minutes, I trudged all the way up those long imposing and dangerous stairs, cautiously seeking not to slip on the slimy, shiny surfaces... and pushed firmly and intentionally on the large glass doors... But alas! To my immediate surprise and frustration, I found the doors were soundly locked and bolted, abruptly resisting my entry! Frankly, I was soon very close to tears. I had invested significant emotional and physical energy to be there that day, but this establishment was closed because it was a public holiday! Grrr!

With hindsight I had wondered and felt strange in that there didn't seem to be anyone around. It was like walking around a lunar landscape. No one milling noisily around the streets, walking, biking, motoring etc., as one would expect in a big city. It was eerily silent. I felt a deep sense of disappointment as I discovered those massively huge doors locked defiantly in my face, mocking my valiant attempt to travel across town to extend my knowledge of this ancient and regal land of England.

Well, there I was wallowing in my disappointment and mulling over my current situation. I soon decided my best option was simply to go back to the hotel and rest for the remainder of the day ready for work tomorrow. So I turned around gingerly and headed back down the stairs. But before I had taken even a few steps both my feet skidded violently from beneath me, as if something had struck them from behind, and I fell suddenly backwards without warning, landing heavily with my shoulder blades and hips striking two separate edges of the stairs. I felt a sharp crack, a stabbing pain and a zap like a bolt of lightning sizzle through my body. My upper and lower body seemed to strike the marble in the same instant, the breath was driven forcefully from my lungs and my mind was alive with a thousand thoughts in the same instant of time. Then as I lay there looking anxiously at the sky, but not really seeing anything, gasping for breath and panting like a winded boxer, who had just been punched in the belly. I soon realized I could not move. No part of my body would respond as I desperately struggled to rise from where I'd fallen. I felt pinned to the ground, immobilized. Then the thoughts began to slow down a little and flow more serially through my consciousness, yet still at an accelerated pace. This could be very serious. I may be crippled or quadriplegic. I might have cracked my spine. I wasn't even sure whether I'd hit my head on the stone steps. I still couldn't move or feel anything. Suddenly a wave of fear came upon me. I could die here and no- one would even know. I couldn't even speak for lack of wind in my lungs. The wave of shock immobilizing my system meant I couldn't even move to attract attention if anyone came by. I could lie here till tomorrow until people come back to work. I may never see my wife and children again in this world. I could be buried here. The intensity of fear and dread increased as the negative thoughts kept on coming. I was becoming captive to the anxiety and worry that was beginning to set in. I could still not move my body, and if I could move what would I do, where could I go? Everyone is on holidays! This was fast looking like a hopeless situation, perhaps the end of life's journey. Self-doubt then began, this was a stupid idea, I should have stayed back at the hotel and none of this would have happened. That's what I get for pushing too hard doing too much. It wasn't worth the effort. Well, this could be it. My life began to flash before my eyes in memories, thoughts of unfinished business and dreams, unfulfilled hopes, unresolved issues, relationships yet to be built and all of the people and things I'd miss, and those who would miss me. It's just not right! Then despair appeared, knocking on the door of my soul as if to say, "Ahah! I have you where I want you now! You're finished! You may as well succumb! Give In!" My heart was beating faster, ominous fear and dread seemed to be taking hold. I was struggling for something positive to hold onto, some hope to cling to. But none was coming to mind. This was an example of the absence of *genuine peace*.

Eventually, I cried out to the Lord and said, "I am yours Lord, deal with me as you will," then something marvellous happened.

All of a sudden, I realized I was breathing a little easier. My heart rate was slowing down somewhat, and I was beginning to feel my body again, although it was still very painful and stiff and not responding as it should. I was also beginning to sense again the presence of that dear friend who has been with me all the days of my life. Slowly some feeling and movement returned to my body, and I was able to cautiously rise to my feet and hobble tentatively down to the bottom of the stairs, clutching tightly to and leaning on the handrails all the way down. Then I thought all I could do was to limp slowly back along the path I had come, towards the train station, hoping things would improve as I went. Well they didn't really, I felt like a stooped little hundred-year-old man racked with a mixture of pain and numbness, still shaking like a leaf from the incident, but a sense of calm was slowly returning, a feeling that everything would be OK.

Can you believe it?! About 500 meters down the road, which I had walked past without realizing, was a fully functioning hospital with all the necessary staff on duty. I shuffled in and explained my plight and they attended to me straight away. They checked all my vitals, aches and pains and such, kept me in observation for an hour or so and then released me saying that I was totally fine, with no residual injuries. My peace returned steadily, and I was able to walk and train home without incident and spent the remainder of the day preparing for our next assignment. What a miracle, what a joy this peace really is. I never want to be without it or have to operate outside that place of *genuine peace.*

I am convinced that even if I had died there that day, this peace would have taken me home in a sublime state of surrender, comfort, rest, hope and joy... And that this readily accessible state of heart and mind, is certainly well worth fighting for, working towards, and passionately seeking to acquire as part of our normal everyday life.

What did I learn that day? I found a new settled peace in knowing that wherever I travelled anywhere in the world His heavenly protection was always with me. That this favour was constantly on my life, and He was always at my side. That the concept of 'accidents' are very real and often contrived by forces outside of ourselves, but they are nevertheless not beyond the purview of heaven, nor beyond His ability to stop them happening, walk with us through them, minimize the potential harm or bring positive outcomes, even out of seemingly negative circumstances. I learned that fear is a negative force outside of ourselves which seeks to strike at the heart of humanity and destroy our resolve and ability to fight for good in life, and the world around us. Fear can immobilize, discourage, oppress and depress, by creating nervousness, anxiety, self-doubt, uncertainty or despair. And such fear is an enemy of peace, and needs to be resisted philosophically, spiritually, mentally and practically on all fronts. To allow fear to enter in or have any part in our lives is a recipe for serious setback, possible failure or even total disaster. But, as already stated, there is a remedy available to each and every one of us!

Chapter 4 - Relationships are the Foundation of Peace

I am blessed to have lived a long, happy and fulfilling life with myriad varieties of learning, across a broad span of issues. I have read, researched, studied, observed, learned and experienced life from so many diverse perspectives and in so many different types of situations, personally and together with friends, colleagues and clients. There are many things I have discovered and observed, and *genuine peace* is one of the most important. I have found that peace is meant to be the ideal and ultimate outcome of all positive human endeavours.

Another is that true peace is only possible within a healthy set of positive, ideally potentially covenant relationships of a variety of different categories. One cannot achieve a comprehensive multifaceted peace without relating to others. It is impossible to do alone. The essence and benefits of peace require input, interrelationships and constructive connections and dialogs with others. Sometimes with people and entities we may never have considered. A reclusive lifestyle for example, while seeming to have some obvious advantages by way of simplicity and the like, often lacks a sufficiently rich web of connections and communication which are possible within a larger more diverse, stretching, supportive and yet challenging network of relationships. This can feel threatening at times, but I have always found it is worth the effort to reach out and seek to build new relationships with others. Even though some such endeavours may seem unproductive at the time, we still acquire so much helpful knowledge and wisdom, about people, and ourselves as well as life, hope, meaning and purpose.

I'm sure you've also heard the truism that it's more about who you know in life rather than what you know. This statement encapsulates the importance of relationship; however, it's not just who you know that matters, it is the quality and type of relationship that you have with them, which is also of critical importance.

My third book Learning Places: Real Love is a valuable resource regarding healthy relationships, but I also add some further information regarding relationships here because it is germane to the topic of peace.

Firstly, it sounds quite simplistic and obvious to say that peace can only begin to be achieved between two parties if they are actually in contact with each other. Some people for various reasons, at times not even known to themselves, will boycott or refuse to even speak with the other person. This kind of behaviour which can be out of innocence, naivety, unkindness or indeed disrespect, maybe even retribution, is a classic destroyer or denier of potential peace. In order for there to be a relationship of any sort, and therefore the possibility for peace between two parties, the first thing to do is seek to meet, even if doing so might be very difficult. If peace is the goal, meeting each other is a critical, some would even say mandatory step on that journey. Of course, great effort can and should be put into seeking to minimize the chances of failure and maximize the chance of success of such meeting. One could choose for example a mutually agreeable location, a pleasant peaceful atmosphere, a simple non-threatening agenda, a meal or snack at no cost, short duration for the meeting, promise of respect and congeniality and each should feel free to bring a supportive friend if they choose. There should always be an easy means of 'escape' when one party feels threatened or too physically, emotionally or spiritually challenged. One should start simple and brief, not expect too much on first meeting and hopefully agree to meet again. If meeting in person is not initially possible, as a starting point, one could perhaps agree to exchange a letter, email or message. One or the other or both parties by arrangement could also agree to appoint a mutually trusted mediator, advocate, witness or go-between to help begin a stalled or stalemated process. The objective is to just begin to talk and become comfortable speaking with each other, even if topics of contention are not initially broached at all. Working on more serious matters can only be done once some rapport and trust are established.

Once the ice is broken, the parties are a little more comfortable with each other, and some sort of dialog has commenced, then the process of building trust can begin. This requires openness, vulnerability, honesty, integrity and transparency at all times on all topics. It's much better to say you don't know or you are uncomfortable or not at liberty to speak about something, than it is to lie, feel intimidated or fabricate scenarios and stories.

There should also always be a willingness to listen, and seek to fully understand, before seeking to be understood.

As trust is extended step by step in a timely way and confidence is slowly built in each other, one can then begin to discuss some issues of increasing importance, which have potential to increase closeness, resolve various matters at issue and generally progress toward reconciliation, and ultimately restoration.

Now you might be thinking at this point that this sounds all too hard. Why should I bother? Who cares if there are a few difficult or unresolved relationships littered through our lives? I must admit I once felt that way, in my younger years, but I have long since learned that it matters very much. As a case in point, if every person in Australia had just one really poor relationship in their lives... there would be at least ten million bad relationships intermingled with each other and scattered through our society. Furthermore, if the existence of one difficult relationship in our lives caused us to be sloppy and uncaring about other relationships before long there would be millions more. This would very quickly get out of hand, add to tension in our communities and ultimately has the potential to breakdown our society. This is typically what causes family disputes, clan wars, and tribal or city conflicts, it can even lead to civil war if things get out of hand. Teaching people to solve and seek to extend and improve problematic relationships, actually adds value and harmony to our societies. Sadly, some life philosophies teach that you just have to be nice to everyone and this issue won't be a problem. If only that were true, but it is not. Being 'nice' to everyone would just leave millions of relationship issues swept under the carpet and not dealt with. This would lead to a myriad of escalating stressful relationships which were not being resolved. Each would steadily get worse, with a flow-on negative effect and escalation across our society.

There are also those who would say that we should ignore differences in values, beliefs, lifestyles and worldviews between individuals, families, groups and sub-groups within our society as well as networks of neighbours and friends. That we should coexist as best we can and just live and let live. This model is also flawed. Firstly, in order to succeed in life, one should at least have a basic well-informed understanding regarding the potential different beliefs and worldviews that exist within our various local and global cultures. This is valuable life knowledge, and if taught comprehensively, with integrity, honesty and non-bias, is extremely healthy for coping socially as individuals and families and helping to make our world a better place. One thing that should be noted at this point is that not all value- systems, lifestyles and cultures are equivalent, some are like cheese and chalk, and each has its strengths, weaknesses, excesses and aberrations. Knowing something about these issues can give critically important capability and opportunity for effective dialog, as well as good understandings and choices. It would give everyone the chance to seriously consider each other's worldviews and values and have the freedom to change to or away from them as we see fit, without implication or retribution. Such an approach would also give our society generally, the necessary information and opportunity to create a set of laws and guidelines which would lead to *genuine peace* for family, community, city and nation. Rather than the current system which seems to arbitrarily dictate from international forums, proposed co- existence methodologies and laws, which often have little or no chance of success, and yet are typically not open for robust, transparent, honest and relevant debate.

Another aspect is that when difficult relationships are not resolved it saps significant emotional and mental energy, which should ideally be applied to other more productive and quality enhancing aspects of life. Consider what it feels like to have a really good value adding, encouraging, mutually beneficial, open, respectful relationship with a close friend. It actually adds value to your life and theirs and even has a very therapeutic effect on our body, soul and spirit. You see, we are designed for relationship, and when we don't have sufficient positive family, friendship and community connections around us our enjoyment of life and well-being suffers. This may seem strange to some, but I have found in my life and the lives of those who have confided in me, that if there is one or more broken relationships somewhere within our network of friends, colleagues or family, that this apparent anomaly causes us pain, deep within our spirit. If we will take the time to focus and reflect on such broken relationships, we will soon feel the sorrow, disappointment, grief, loss, regret, hurt rejection or other such pivotal emotions and thoughts... initially on our own behalf... But then, if we have the compassion, patience and courage, to linger a little longer. And reflect on the feelings of the other party... we will begin to see, feel, sense, observe, assume or deduce that similar types of experiences are also occurring in the other person's spirit, as a result of this brokenness. I discern that this is clear evidence of there being a deep longing within our soul and spirit to be at peace with others. Furthermore, if we neglect to attempt to resolve these broken relationships or at least to do our part toward resolution, then we will continue to suffer these 'wounds' in our spirit indefinitely. This unhealthy disturbance in our being will have an adverse effect on the quality and enjoyment of our lives. Sadly, some even take these broken relationships to the grave. This really breaks my heart!

It should be noted as well that too many broken or difficult relationships remaining unresolved within our lives can be very debilitating, even destructive, and can in fact be a primary root cause of oppression, depression and even suicide.

Then there are those relationships where you have tried everything to resolve but nothing seems to work. Even these seemingly interminable situations can potentially and ultimately be resolved, and the emotional and stress levels managed, until such a time as they are restored. The most important aspect is to keep blessing, praying for and desiring the best possible outcome for this relationship and the other person involved. It means that insomuch as it depends on you, to always be maintaining a positive attitude, keeping the door open and the invite hanging out there for contact to be made and matters resolved whenever they are ready. The Good Book says that as far as it depends on us, we should or can be at peace with all people and can even have peace with our enemies! And most astoundingly, that heaven is powerfully and persistently on our side, in order to achieve this outcome. It is not some impossible dream, but rather an ideal to be pursued with determination in life.

Chapter 5 - Life Categories, Boundaries, Interactions and Characteristics

This chapter is structured around a defined list of various key life categories, which are individuals and groups of people that I have distilled, as being natural building blocks to help describe how the goal of *genuine peace* may be achieved in society. It also includes some of the characteristics of each life category, the boundaries which need to be in place for healthy peaceful relationships, and the various types of interactions which need to occur.

Firstly I present:-
- The concept of boundaries between the domains of each life category;
- Why these boundaries are important;
- What typically happens when the boundaries are not fully developed;
- Why it's important that the inner aspects of each life category are mature and effective;
- Which features are common to positive life category connections; and
- Which usually cause negative connections and therefore disturb the peace;
- Then finally, the various life categories are each listed and considered individually, regarding their unique and/or similar characteristics, with emphasis on those aspects which will significantly and necessarily enhance peace in each domain.

I should also clarify here that I'm not suggesting that relationships must be resolved blindly, in a superficial fashion or at any cost. This will achieve nothing of lasting value. Good healthy relationships, which have the potential to embody the concept of *genuine peace*, require for example positive values, beliefs, boundaries and worldview, as well as love, joy, patience, kindness, goodness, respect, honour, faithfulness and self-control, just to mention a few. It is also ideal if these can be shared and held in common between the parties, although that is not always possible. Without such positive character traits and attitudes, problems cannot be properly resolved, or relationships effectively maintained.

Let's begin with life category boundaries. They are important and critical aspects of any relationship. I will use this term to describe the behavioural rules, guidelines, principles, understandings, perimeters, norms, protections and safety nets, etc. which occur at the boundary of each life category. These can be optional, negotiable or non-negotiable depending on their nature, yet are or should be involved in every human relationship. Such concepts are germane to achieving sound resolution of broken relationships, as well as being imperative for the healthy ongoing maintenance of generally good relationships.

There are a series of sound and wise foundational boundaries which apply to all relationships and there are others which are unique and specific to various categories. Life categories are for example individuals, husbands and wives, de-facto couples, families, parent and child, siblings, extended family, churches, small groups, affinity groups, clubs and societies, communities, neighbourhoods, workplaces, culture groups, nations, bilateral nation to nation, nation trading groups, and all-nation internationally.

Every life category type can be considered to have its own dominion-boundary which encircles the particular entity in its entirety and defines its geography, edge and extents. All forms of interaction between life category types occur through these boundaries. The ideal is that each dominion boundary is mature, functional and sufficiently developed to cater for the congenial and effective functioning of all necessary and appropriate types of interaction. There needs to be comfortable, agreed and mutually beneficial protocols, language and methods which cater for every possibility of interchange. However, when some new type of interaction is attempted, for example were conversation needs to move to a deeper more personal or vulnerable level, there also needs to be the ability to develop new boundary navigation models 'on the fly', without having to temporarily suspend the relationship or cause major disruption or dislocation. In a human interaction sense, some of these skills come more naturally to some people than to others. Most can be learned with the commensurate time and effort, providing effective teachers, mentors, training and resources are available. When these mature dominion boundary functionalities can be developed and maintained, a healthy level of *genuine peace* can be maintained. If not, there will always be constant or periodic tensions, stresses and difficulties at the boundaries of relationships.

Furthermore, **if life category dominion boundaries are under-developed,** trying to interact through them often creates inordinate pain for one or both parties. Examples of such are as follows: 1) Depending on the complexity, timing, need, or urgency of an interaction, one could try to *crash through* like a bull at a gate, 2) Endeavor to undermine, create doubt or instil a lack of confidence, then try to *go through beneath the gateway* in a sneaky insincere fashion. 3) Make an attempt to find a loophole or flaw in the boundary and seek to *drive wedges* into the gaps, weakening the integrity of the interface. 4) Totally avoid the boundary as if it was not there and try to *usurp, dominate, and intimidate* one's way over the top.

It should be noted at this point that in order to have mature peaceful interactions at the boundaries, **the internal aspects of life category entities also need to be mature**, healthy and well developed. This is a non-trivial problem in that each entity will have its own internal functionality, ideas, aspects, boundaries, issues and modes of interaction, which are usually under the exclusive control of the entity in question. Change can then typically only be made by life category entities and sub entities themselves. This challenge requires access to information, education, training and role models but also typically depends on the willingness of individuals in their own right and as part of various group entities, to have the desire to change and improve, and be willing to make the effort and sacrifice required. This is one of society's most grave dilemmas. Good behaviour cannot typically be brought about by legislation. Such outcomes require a constructive attitude and often a change of heart in the individuals involved. Changes of heart in turn require a positive, often newly acquired, and internalized, worldview and set of related beliefs and values.

General boundaries and interaction characteristics which are common and typically required to achieve positive connection and *genuine peace* between any and all types of life category are firstly, some basic degree of respect, honour, truth, honesty, openness, transparency, integrity and patience. Plus, a genuine desire to listen and understand, as well as persistence, self-control and a sense of value and worth, for self and the other party. There also obviously needs to be a willingness to first of all meet, then to seek constructive dialog, while always maintaining a desire to do the right thing and make the particular circumstances, and the world at large, a much better place for all. These basic motives, attitudes and methods will set a strong foundation for any type of human interfacing. However, their absence, to varying degrees, can make peaceful interaction problematic or even worse still, impossible.

I should also mention at this point that there are numerous negative behaviours which also inhibit or may even negate the possibility of *genuine peace* and **should never be occurring** at any of the relationship category boundaries. They are for example dishonour, disrespect, denigration, abuse, mocking, intimidation, vilification, lying, stealing, embezzlement, confusing, creating chaos, manipulation, controlling, adultery, taking sexual advantage, torture, terror and murder. If we wish to achieve anything of real importance in life and relationships, we need to remove these concepts from our human interactions... And, I might add, we can be assured that this type of positive approach is potentially possible, because most rational people would deem this normal and desirable behaviour, and that when achieved in sufficient numbers and quality, will truly make the world a much better place.

Now for some examples of aspects which are typically unique or different between particular life category- entities and their respective boundaries and relationships:-

1) Husband and wife - This relationship goes beyond the bounds of normal human love and friendship. There is a deep abiding love, intimacy, oneness and mutuality, meant to be present in covenant marriage between a man and a woman. They are also meant to operate as a close and effective team to nurture, provide for, love, protect and prepare their children for life and eternity... As well as being uniquely designed to lead and nurture the family unit to provide a sound and wise building block of society. This is the most intricate, intimate, complex, sophisticated, vulnerable, supportive and potentially mutually beneficial earthly relationship of all. This is the person with whom ideally, one will spend the lion's share of time on the journey of life. They will share to one degree or another, the bed, the bedroom, bathroom, and facilities. Food, money, home, garden, vehicles, children, logistics, recreation, hobbies and holidays; together with dreams, goals, mission, calling, passions and life in general, are all common territory to be shared closely with one another. It is so worth the effort to work diligently towards the best possible, high quality, loving, respectful, honouring, mutually beneficial interactions, dialogs and relationship outcomes. Level setting and getting to know and enjoy each other fully and completely; communicating, sharing, understanding, resolving issues personally and as a couple are pure gold and bring so many benefits mutually and as individuals. Once knowing each other fully, and being fully known, we can work out optimal boundaries and methods of operation, gifting and interest. Some things will be shared together and there will always be room to grow and explore areas individually as well. Achieving *genuine peace* at this level is critical to the wellbeing and enjoyment of individuals in marriage, and in life generally, and ultimately positively benefits the family and the whole of humanity. I should also add that due to a variety of life choices, directions and circumstances there is always the possibility of more than one marriage in a lifetime. Observation and experience in this area has shown that the best approach to achieving maximum success and enjoyment is that even though often much more complex than a first marriage, the new relationship should be treated with the same solemnity, diligence, love and faithfulness as a first marriage.

2) De-facto couple male - female - These relationships are an unofficial equivalent of a married couple, usually entered into without any form of ritual, legal or covenant commitment. In order to work well they therefore potentially require all of the relationship and boundary functionality, variety, complexity and sophistication of the husband-and-wife couple above, yet usually lack the prior moral, personal and legal agreement related there to. De-facto relationships of their very nature therefore often lack stability, durability and enduring peace because of the uncertainty in which they have been entered into. In fact, in many cultures more than 80% will fail. It should be noted too that in many nations once a couple have cohabitated for a reasonable period of time they are deemed to be and usually treated in most aspects under law, as if they were a married couple anyway. This can be a surprise to many and can bring a quagmire of legal and practical challenges. However, if one finds oneself in a de-facto male - female relationship and it is enjoyable, fulfilling and has potential for marriage and family in the future, then the same principles espoused for marriage, should be applied, to give the relationship every chance of strategic success.

3) Family - Consists of the biological parents, together with their blood-born children and includes the husband and wife, parent and child, and sibling to sibling relationship and boundary types. It is a unique, complex and sophisticated network of relationships which together form imperative and critical foundational building blocks for society. Family is a natural extension of the husband - wife life entity explored above. The foundational relationships between the couple remain the same, but they become more complex with the overlay of children having been added to the equation. Parent and child relationships are as myriad as the personalities and issues of each individual and the internal and external relationships, influences, circumstances and life experiences. In addition to the common characteristics mentioned above like honouring and respecting each other, which are critical to successful family relationships, there is also the need to work as a team. The family unit is the most fundamental and foundational of social teams required in a healthy society, and family members need to work together in order to survive and prosper as individuals and as a cohesive unit. Their survival then gives all other entities with which they interact or are associated, a much greater chance of success. Healthy families bring about strong healthy societies and nations. But wait, I have digressed somewhat, let's back up a little and start from the beginning. Children when first born need to bond with both a father and a mother and grow in congenial, loving, nurturing, relationship with both of them ideally, in order to develop naturally and fully into mature and wise male or female adults, according to their chromosome configuration at birth... This fact has been lost in some of the more recent flawed attempts at socially reengineering the family unit. All children need to have a quality relationship with both their mother and father, who themselves need to be positive role models. This is necessary for the developing child to experience and learn how to be a good mother or father themselves, as per their birth gender. They will ideally at least, also learn some of the critical and fundamental skills required to be an effective parent and spousal partner in marriage. I'm sure you've heard of the saying that 'blood is thinker than water'. This saying applies practically and descriptively to the family unit as well. It refers to the fact that because the husband and wife are committed to a lifelong bond, and the children, who are in effect the fruit of this relationship, are a creative hybrid combination of the genes of both their parents, they in a very practical sense 'share the same blood' and have a common heritage-bond, and ancestry line from which they have come. This in and of itself creates a very real and robust familial, collegial, biological, scientific, relational and human connection between family members. Furthermore, in most cases they have grown up together, shared many life experiences and great learning, both positive and beneficial, but also potentially risky and often life threatening. When these situations are managed well, they build a very powerful sense of belonging and shared adventure, suffering, perseverance and sustained human endeavour, which is unequalled in Nature, and creates a potentially durable, positive and cohesive social entity, which is at the heart of every strong, mature and effective society. One cannot over emphasize the benefits of developing and maintaining well-functioning family units which enjoy a generous level of *genuine peace*. Adoption and fostering into healthy family units can also be used to help compensate for children and individuals who find themselves in difficult or unsatisfactory family situations, and this usually helps them cope and develop much better, both personally and as fellow contributors to society. It should be noted however that accommodating, encouraging, or purposely seeking to create experimental or alternative style family units does not usually add value or improve quality of family life. In fact, some hybrid types are so 'left-field' that they can actually physically, psychologically, socially or emotionally damage individual family members, often quite seriously. This area is worthy of significant further study, objective discussion and resolution in order to stem ideological attacks on the tried and true natural family model. I should also reiterate that this book for the sake of expediency and achieving optimal outcomes focuses mainly on describing the ideal approaches to *genuine peace*, because they are typically designed to achieve best results. However, as space allows and thought and analysis processes guide, I have also sought to include other helpful information regarding various alternatives.

4) Parent and child - Father and mother relationships with children. - This type of relationship is clearly a subset of family, and some aspects have been touched on in that segment above. Some other additional unique and special characteristics of this relationship which require attention in order to achieve *genuine peace* are for example, a child needs and often craves the friendship, support, affirmation, example, encouragement, mentoring and tutoring of both gender parents, as well as assistance and guidance with the setting of life boundaries, principles, values, beliefs and a healthy sense of right and wrong. Discipline is necessary on occasion, ideally by way of a combination of reward and loss of privileges, depending on the appropriateness of the child's behaviour. Some have suggested that one can raise a child without discipline, or without even saying "no" to them, but sadly in the majority of cases this has not worked. Lack of discipline leads to self-centred, self-seeking, self-serving, even rebellious behaviour toward life and authority figures. This can make it very difficult for some to adjust to working life, and all adult life and family relationships. In the workplace for example there is always a need and expectation of good, responsible, hardworking, customer focused behaviour. One is always required to toe the line, do what is asked, work with the team and achieve the job goals. If these life skills are not learned in childhood a person will have extreme difficulty in holding down a steady job or career, establishing a strong positive home life or starting a family, etc. All of which require a high level of discipline, perseverance, self-control and a healthy others'-centred approach to life generally. It is also typically the parents who are best positioned to pass on the essence of these skills together with a robust and viable worldview to their children. Public education systems are not able to do this well, they should simply reinforce the basic Judeo-Christian values which are the foundation of every safe, secure, happy, effective, productive, positive, growing, developing, free and just society. There should never be attempts made to hybridize radically different sets of values and beliefs together into one society. This is fraught with problems, simply does not work effectively and serves to confuse the next generation of children born to a nation. This is typically what precipitates social tension, frustration, strife, anger, violence, conflict, and draconian, authoritarian attempts to keep peace and enforce certain behaviour. In extreme cases if left unchecked this social strategy can lead to civil war or 'clashes of civilizations', none of which are desirable in a healthy city, state or nation. There is more information and rationale on this preferred and optimal worldview issue necessarily contained in other sections. It is also needful to mention here too that due to life choices and circumstances, broken marriages, families and the death of spouses, parents and children etc., many of us will find ourselves as widows, widowers, divorcees, single parents, stepchildren, or orphans on the journey of life. This is not ideal but is often, in fact usually, outside of our control and sphere of influence and is another key type of challenge we each have to face in life. Much has been offered on these topics in my earlier books and I feel the need to add the following. Observation, learning and experience in these situations, and in relation to the goal of achieving *genuine peace* in our lives and society, is that in order to achieve optimal outcomes we still need to seek to apply all the general peace principles articulated throughout this book including:- a) Placing our relationship with God as our highest priority and taking His lead and guiding as to how best to navigate through the particular circumstances of our own life; b) Seeking to achieve the best attributes of the optimal outcomes described here in, by for example being willing to step into various appropriate roles in order to help others compensate for their less than ideal or problematic life situations, including allowing others to help us in similar fashion; c) For example offering to be a responsible part time supportive male or female role model to children; d) Giving practical help, friendship and support to single parents, widows, widowers etc; e) Seeking to be a responsible and loving step- mum or step-dad to children where that is needed or desired; f) While continuing to honour your natural dad or mum always be respectful and honouring to those who may have become your step-mum or step-dad; g) And work with and enjoy fellowship among your most positive other life category group/s, for example your church, to leverage the power of community and to help compensate for any lack or broken relationships there may currently be in the family; h) And finally, seek to hope for the best, and work toward the best possible outcomes with prayer, patience, faith, love and action, leaving the rest in God's hands.

5) Sibling to sibling - Brothers and sisters amongst themselves. These relationships are also a subset of family, and the quality of sibling relationships are critically important to achieving *genuine peace* as well. I'm sure you have seen situations where brothers and sisters may fight like cats and dogs in the privacy and safety of their own home. Yet when faced with a common threat outside, will galvanize into a strong cohesive family unit, stand up together and mount a concerted effort to protect, defend and advocate for the one who is at risk. Often without fear for their own personal safety or reputation. While not an ideal example, since brothers and sisters ought to develop the skill and discipline of consistently loving and honouring each other no matter where they are. It is nevertheless a good general example of how siblings should be positive toward each other, seek to guide, help, and support and encourage each other, with wisdom and compassion, always being there for each other. When parents ultimately die the strength, cohesion and quality of sibling relationships are what govern how well the family will do after their parents have gone. These relationships are therefore also critical for *genuine peace* within the family, the community and the nation. Over history it is often the strong families (clans) which have formed the backbone of cities, states and nations and ultimately guide and govern their future destiny. And finally, step- brothers and step-sisters while always seeking to pay attention to and improve the quality and cohesion of their own natural sibling relationships, should also seek to reach out in compassion and friendship to their newly acquired brothers and sisters. Closer cohesion of blended siblings is usually more appropriate and achievable when the families are melded through marriage while the children are at a very young age.

6) Extended family - Uncles, aunts, cousins, grandparents, grandchildren, great grandparents etc. This broader family once again embodies and benefits from, or indeed suffers, due the quality, or lack thereof, in all of the above relationships. Have you ever seen a movie where an Italian family clan gathers together for a special family occasion? It always excites me to see what a large gathering it is and the camaraderie and carnival atmosphere. Even if there is bad blood between some, they usually try to forget it on the day and put the issues aside and enter into the joy of the occasion. Whether it is Christmas, Easter or a family wedding. These are examples of what should be high points on any family calendar. **Christmas**, the day we celebrate Jesus Christ came from heaven to earth as a tiny baby, born of a virgin, to experience all that we do as human beings here on earth, and prepare to give his life as the price for our sins, that we might have the potential to enter into heavenly rest with him. **Easter**, when he was cruelly and illegally arrested, tortured and murdered on a cross. Then on the third day He rose again after having conquered satan, hell and death, and showed himself as a witness to many, then returned in the clouds to Glory to advocate on our behalf at the right hand of God. And finally, a **Wedding**, which is the kernel relationship of an earthly family, modelled on the relationship we are meant to have with God our

Saviour, as an outworking of Christmas and Easter. If we would seriously apply the redemptive, healing life changing power which is manifest in these three pivotal covenant occasions in our lives and families what an amazing enjoyable world this would be... filled with *genuine peace*, joy, faith, hope, love and fellowship. My third book Learning Places: Real Love contains volumes of helpful information and testimony to expand on some of these topics. I know from firsthand experience that what I'm suggesting here is eminently feasible. It is possible to have healthy, enjoyable relationships, wonderful satisfying fulfilling marriages and families. The how-to information is available. The role models exist. Redemptive heavenly support is available. We just need the will and determination to have the best, and not be satisfied with the mediocre. We need to be willing to work on our relationships in both directions, always seeking harmony, reconciliation and restoration. In the majority of cases, it is possible. We usually fail because we don't have the will to succeed, and one or the other of the parties refuses to engage toward recovery. But even if there are one or two broken relationships within an extended family, a strong healthy family will support the ones who are struggling to succeed or will alternatively help them to cope with any brokenness. This gives them time and opportunity to find true healing and often another chance, all the while protecting, nurturing and assisting them to recover and go on with life, making the best of what they have. The larger extended family often has people of numerous different personalities, myriads of life skills, gifting, wisdom and talents, all of which can potentially be applied to solving the challenges of individuals in the family unit. This is the true power of family. Regarding achieving *genuine peace* in broken relationships between large extended families or developing clans, it is almost impossible to meld two really large established family units. It would have to be a 'takeover' as it were... Yet I feel compelled to suggest that there always needs to be one or more good hearted and Godly peacemakers on the scene. They will be prepared to pay the price to help hold onto, maintain and develop any vestige of relationships that exist, or should do so, between their original clan, and the one of which they have recently become a part. This sacrificial act will be used of God to help engender a better quality peace over time. I commend the courageous folk who have the opportunity and determination to consider this task. God will show who the best candidates to fulfill these roles will be, and they too will help make the world a better place.

7) Churches - Ecclesia 'families' of believers in and followers of Jehovah God and the Lord Jesus Christ. This is an earthly representation of the heavenly family of believers and disciples of Jesus. It has been called the Body of Christ or the Family of God, for good reason and should ideally be an oasis of *genuine peace*. Sadly, this is not always the case. However, passionately applying and living out the principles in His Book, under the guidance of His Holy Spirit, does make it possible to be so. The church is also a blessed place for individuals who for whatever reason do not have family of their own, or do not have positive, functional family members with whom they can fellowship. Once again much has been said about the church community in my earlier books, but for the purpose of this topic I need to add a few additional thoughts. For example, it would not be possible to have *genuine peace* here on earth without the church being present. Even with all its short comings and flaws and though it seems to receive endless criticisms from all and sundry, including sadly those within its own ranks, and sadder still those who simply have no idea, or firsthand knowledge of the church on which to base such complaint. Two thousand years ago Jesus left a deposit of His Holy Spirit in human vessels here on earth, and charged them and their followers, to spread this powerful all-loving Gospel of *genuine peace*, throughout the generations and across the whole earth, until all have heard and had opportunity to receive Him, and the perfect peace which can only be found in Him. The Judeo-Christian church across the whole earth is meant to operate in federation under the guidance of King Jesus, to fully achieve this goal, before He can return to earth, as He promised He would. There are however dark forces seeking to inhibit this process, to take this earthly kingdom for their own ends, and to usurp the kingdom away from the true victorious returning King Jesus. But the church and those who are and will become followers of King Jesus, are an invincible truly positive force, protecting and seeking to lead, guide and govern our world, maybe even our universe, for good. They thereby defend it from the perversions of darkness, which seek to dominate, consume and destroy. If you look carefully and intently, with your mind's eye into the events of our generation, seeking heavenly revelation, and to identify the root causes of our real problems, you will eventually perceive this truth. You will begin to see the perversions and aberrations being unleashed upon our civilization as being 'normal', or acceptable, and hopefully will realize their deleterious effects and choose to support and join the army of the Kingdom of God to seek to resist them.

8) Small group - Small churches or elements of a church. These small groups are the working teams, the 'battle units' of the wider church. It is difficult to do many things as a large group. Most human endeavours which add value, have emanated from small groups of passionate believers, who will put their all on the line in support of a cause, which they deem more important than their own comfort, well-being and reputation. God is using such groups again, en-masse in His church, in order to accelerate and increase intensity in areas which He deems important in our time. We need to be listening for His still small voice and be willing to work with such groups of like-minded campaigners in order to save humankind. As I write this it sounds like some classic science fiction epic... yet I know in my heart that this is practical, purposeful and true in our time. There is a sense of urgency in my spirit that God is raising up a Seventh Column to both resist the darkness and to bring the Light of God to the earth. Please consider.

9) Affinity group - A group of people with similar interests. These gatherings are prevalent in our society and comprise those with a common interest coming together formally or informally to create a group with a common set of goals and objectives. Our society is made up of hundreds of thousands of such groups. My life learning here is that in order to achieve *genuine peace* in our society, our cities and our nation such groups need to have only, or mostly positive, constructive uplifting intentions and practical goals and projects. In our type of society however we seek to be a free country and give citizens as much choice as possible. Obviously, everyone just can't be allowed to do whatever they please. There are some seriously evil people in the world who are often being driven by some hideous demons, and love evil, resist good, and enjoy hurting people. The challenge is to decide reasonably what should be allowed and what shouldn't, in a fair, just and rational manner. In a Judeo-Christian western country, there are generally righteous rules in law which govern good behaviour and guide decisions like this, as to whether they are in the best interest of society. These are of some assistance in deciding which groups to ban. However, there are an increasing number of fringe laws based on various flawed socialist and other philosophical models, which are beginning to seek to put laws on our books that are questionable, and drive attempts at creating new norms, or human rights, etc. These often do not add value to society but rather create confusion, or chaos, by for example undermining positive norms, taboos, traditions, groups or behaviours which have served society for generations. Sadly, the proponents of such changes typically have not thought through as to what the logical outcomes would be, before placing them into law. Or worse still I suspect some have been purposely placed in the legal system to create chaos and confusion, as an excuse or enabler, seeking to justify larger more draconian government structures and laws. One strategy I'd like to suggest which would address some of the root causes and foundational issues in the area of affinity groups is that good hearted, well-intended Godly leaders in the community both male and female, young and older should rise up and create all manner of positive affinity groups which would add value to society and engender *genuine peace*. This would be in order that there were so many groups on such a broad scale of interest that they would cover the needs and interests of most citizens. Leaders would also need to make sure the groups are governed with good, Godly, uplifting values which would actually help mentor and train people in positive life and relationship skills that would naturally make the world a better place. Even groups of a 'fringy' nature could be created and positioned for those with fringe interests, however, be done in a way which makes sure people are not led away to the darker side of that fringe area, but rather be moved toward and remain in the Light. There may still have to be some banned groups, however given that efforts are also made to ensure that our laws are based on sound values and beliefs, disallowed contact groups would be fully justified and generally accepted as being in the best interest of society.

10) Club and society - Sporting, social related or charity entities. These groups are a special instance of a large, pervasive, oft-cloned affinity group created in domains like sports, charities and other areas of great social need. Thoughts above would therefore also apply. Many of the most successful and beneficial groups in this area have been started over the years as part of church groups, with all the positive social, and spiritual benefits arising there-from. Sadly, some groups have grown so massively and become powers and businesses unto themselves. However as long as they are governed by good and Godly principles and leaders, and their specialist area of interest is not draconian but rather adding value to society, they do have the potential to engender *genuine peace*. Sport for example gives adventurous, athletic, competitive, young people an outlet where they can focus these energies positively. They are taught to operate within rules and guidelines which teach them positive life skills, as well as minimizing collateral damage, and helping to keep some people out of trouble and 'off the street'. This is a valuable addition to society. Many other groups which also meet the needs of youth, seniors, men and women respectively are all becoming pervasive, are led by good hearted people, and are adding positively to our society, and the harmony thereof. In the interest of general wellbeing groups of this type should ideally also have a chaplain at their disposal, to deal with matters of the heart and spirit like life stresses, personal challenges, grief, loss, crisis, trauma, relationship tensions and such.

11) Community - A loosely coupled network of people, usually living in a local area. The above principles also apply to this category. Community groups can be, for example, retirement villages, intentional shared communities, university campuses, boarding schools and the like. In the interest of healthy community life these groups should have access to common facilities large enough to gather as a total group or in small affinity groups. Sports, exercise, healthy lifestyle, social groups, craft, painting, writing, reading, debating, researching, lobbying, educational activities etc., should typically be available as needed and according to group interest. Leaders of groups should be good and Godly with mature life and leadership skills to keep the groups positive and focused on worthwhile and constructive endeavours. Chaplains should also be available and church services and prayer groups on a regular basis. Offering to help practically and pray for peoples' needs are also key.

12) Neighbourhood - Groups of neighbours in a local street. These relationship groups are a little more ad hoc and difficult to develop but there is a genuine need in order to maintain a healthy, peaceful society. In every street, in each town, village or city there lives a variety of people with different backgrounds, life circumstances, needs and issues. Some are lonely, fearful, lacking resources, unsure about their future, facing life crises, dealing with bad relationships, struggling to pay the rent, the mortgage or the bills. Some don't have the life skills they need, can't read or write English; don't understand the society in which they live, or the services available to them. Others are struggling to raise children in a foreign environment. Some may even be being abused, harassed, blackmailed etc. Ideally, there needs to be at least one person, family or a small group of good-hearted people who have a genuine concern for their street and the people who live there. They should ideally begin to pray for their neighbours and seek to meet them briefly. Getting to know them without intruding uninvited or unnecessarily into their lives. Obtaining names and a small part of their life story is important so one can slowly become aware of needs and interests. Then visit occasionally just to say hello and see how they are doing and be prepared to share some of your own story. Such caring people will ultimately become like chaplains, pastors in the street and begin to look out for the various individuals and groups in the neighbourhood. This could then progress to assisting people where they have needs and introducing them to like-minded neighbours if they are interested. Always seeking to build and strengthen harmony, community, knowledge, life skills, Godliness and *genuine peace* in the neighbourhood and street. Sometimes in streets with very industrious and creative facilitators this can end up in all sorts of exciting, enjoyable and productive shared activities and projects like street prayer and fellowship groups, gardening, chess, music, dancing, children playing, craft, sewing, helping each other with chores, doing Christmas lights or having street celebrations. The degree of activity is not as important as the fact that this type of neighbourhood caring is actually happening, with healthy and positive intention, at some level or another. Due to busyness and so many other distractions in life, this function is usually seriously lacking in most neighbourhoods, yet it is greatly needed in order to seriously bring a reasonable level of peace to our societies.

13) Workplace - Everyone's work, profession or vocation. All family members are ultimately involved in learning or working in one way or another, either paid or voluntarily. Because these activities typically make up such a large part of life it's important that *genuine peace* is sought after and hopefully found in those environments. My experience is that with the right attitude it is possible to achieve, as well as seek to maintain, a general peace and wellbeing in the workplace. Firstly, it's important to note that work is not a curse, as some would suggest, but rather a redeemed and sacred life-privilege, which is meant to be beneficial to men, women and children alike, and can and should be satisfying, uplifting, fulfilling and enjoyable. In order to make this readily achievable, the workplace should ideally be based upon a wholesome, servant attitude. An institution should generally exist and be operated with a sense of stewardship toward God and to improve the world at large. All stakeholders including owners, shareholders, staff, suppliers, manufacturers, distributors and customers, should be treated fairly and well, with one not being unduly favoured over another. Work should be celebrated as a joy and outworked with a sense of ministry, destiny, purpose and selflessness. The satisfaction of one' s customers and the success of the business should be taken as personal goals by all, and when challenges are faced, be addressed as a cohesive team. If one staff member is suffering, the others will compassionately seek to help provide moral and practical support and encouragement. The workplace should be looked forward to as a positive extension of personal and home life. It should add quality and enjoyment, and work life balance should be always managed wisely, fairly and well for all parties. Workplace disputes should become unnecessary, because unions should be committed to the balanced and just wellbeing of all, including owners and workers. Staff and other stakeholders should be well informed with openness, transparency, honesty and integrity, and feel adequately included in key decision-making processes. Salaries and conditions should be negotiated reasonably and confidentially and all feel valued and rewarded. When the workplace prospers over and above the norm, profits should be shared to some degree by way of special bonuses, dividends, etc. When a culture like this is fostered broadly across a community, city or Nation, *genuine peace* will begin to flourish.

14) Culture group - Other-language groups from another original culture. Often culture groups voluntarily or forcefully located in other regions remain even more cohesive than in the area from which they initially came. This occurs naturally since people with a common language, heritage and culture may find a common interest in needing to establish and survive in a new, sometimes foreign, cultural, political or geographic context. Having spent time in more than forty countries, and experienced many more different culture groups during my lifetime, I have observed the following:-. In order to achieve resettlement well, with maximum chance of success, including ideal peaceful outcomes, careful attention is required to some basic issues. Depending on the level and nature of difference between the co-existing culture group and the culture they now find themselves residing in, there may need to be some often difficult decisions made by the group. For example, most basic family related issues are common enough to not cause any practical challenges. However, when a custom of the culture group in the new context is deemed illegal, even criminal... then the possibility of compromise or even total change needs to be seriously considered. Because unless the culture group is only transient and remaining in this new location for a short time, the laws, values, beliefs and norms of some new group will quickly be seen to conflict with that of the local area and these types of difference often create irreconcilable sometimes destructive conflict. Some changes are only cosmetic allowing easy compromise, while others are deeply pervasive, intransigent and important to the culture. It is not wise however to assume, allow or encourage the new/visitor culture group to seek to dominate and change the host group by force or subterfuge. This is a form of cultural arrogance which is usually never resolved peacefully. It is fine to believe that one's culture and beliefs are superior to others, as long as we are open to allowing our beliefs and values to be transparently, honestly and fairly discussed, analysed, researched, debated, tested and reflected upon by all enquirers or indeed antagonists, without the need to take offence or resort to curses, threats or violence. Such behaviour leads nowhere positive. All cultures should be open to objective discussion regarding strengths and weaknesses without fear, favour or bias and allow adherents and critics to evolve or change cultures and beliefs as they feel led, hopefully through rational, logical and thoughtful reflection. This single action alone, while creating some initial healthy tension, would ultimately bring positive, peaceful desirable outcomes which would make our towns, cities and nations much more gracious, peaceful and positive, places to live.

15) Nation - A sovereign group of citizens living in a particular geographic area recognized in antiquity and/or in the current day as a nation. These are typically made up of one or more culture groups as defined above, and the observations mentioned there also apply at the national level. **Circumspect wisdom and analysis need to be applied when seeking to decide what culture should be encouraged or**

allowed to dominate in a nation. Some are much more viable, robust and practical, and bring about much better social outcomes than others. Contrary to the opinions of some, allowing multiple conflicting cultures equal status in a nation does not work. This was referred to as **multiculturalism and all attempts to implement this model have failed** or are in the process of failing. I should say at this point the concepts of secularism; humanism, consumerism, materialism, and relativism, have also failed humanity, to one degree or another, as viable, workable social concepts for a healthy nation. **Secularism**: fails because it seeks to remove God, so any righteous intent or heavenly blessing is lost from the marketplace. **Humanism**: because it seeks to elevate man to become his own god, of which we are obviously incapable. **Consumerism**: because the constant acquisition of goods and services does not bring true happiness. **Materialism**: because the ownership of many things does not bring *genuine peace*. And **Relativism**: since not all concepts are of equal worth and there certainly are absolute truths in this universe, without which we would not survive or be able to grow, develop and find new knowledge, or be confident in science, mathematics, space travel, logic and rational thinking etc. I'm sure the creators of these social concepts had high hopes for their success, but they have all fallen so far short, and even though they will always exist to some degree or another there is no true happiness or *genuine peace* to be found therein. **Nations also have systems of government** on which they rely to operate as a society. Some of these have also proven to be more effective than others. For example, **Communism failed** due to lack of healthy competition between businesses, or incentive for workers to work hard, with only limited ability to better oneself, and ultimately because it too sought to eradicate God from its culture. This then removed any potential to discover meaning, purpose or self-worth, while also denying citizens the assistance they need to find personal peace, to resist the forces of darkness, and to receive the benefits and blessings which naturally flow from honouring and serving God. Authoritarian governments on the other hand may succeed while there is a benevolent leader in power, who lives by sound positive good-hearted values, shares wealth effectively among the people, does not make the same errors which communism has typically done, but rather allows citizens the privilege of personal betterment and the freedom to seek and know God. Authoritarian governments also need to have strong, united and often draconian security, police and military capabilities to effectively enforce law and order, which can also be used to destabilize the peace of neighbours. However, such governments quickly fail when a less desirable or evil hearted leader gains power. Nations also clearly have common **character traits, gifts, talents, cultural norms, natural resources, industries and life skills, some good**, and some not so good. The good ones are meant to be capitalized upon and the not-so-good ones redeemed for honourable purposes, but all are meant to be used for the betterment of the particular nation and so that each nation has something to offer to the other nations of the earth. **Finally, I have discovered as have many hundreds of millions of others that for a nation to be strong, viable, consistent, free, just and fair, and for its citizens to be willingly peaceful and congenial with each other and respectfully and**

joyfully engaged and compliant with its laws... the constitution, government, legal system, education system, defence, police and security forces, as well as media, business, economy, church and family models should all be based upon the Judeo-Christian way. Although some have allowed or even encouraged this way of life to be somewhat watered down, diluted or polluted over time, generally speaking the most desired countries in the world, where people clamour to live, are western nations, whose worldview and way of life is founded strongly on an accurate interpretation and implementation of this philosophy. Other nations which seem to prosper but may not yet refer to themselves as being Judeo-Christian usually do so because they have willingly or reluctantly allowed or encouraged the Judeo- Christian way to prosper and spread within their borders... or at very least seek to use some of the basic principles in commerce and life. **This begins to allow the blessings of God to flow upon the nation.**

16) Bilateral Nation to Nation - Any two nations working together for mutually beneficial trade and security. As previously stated, every nation seems to inherently have something of value in and of itself and to potentially share with others. I believe this is by intent and design, rather than by chance, with a view to causing the nations to need each other and to have a desire to work together for the benefit of themselves and others. This has caused the concept of international trade to emerge and become a mainstream form of work and enterprise for the human race. The initial implementation of which has been bilateral, one-to-one trading, because that was easier to manage before the advent of our twentieth century technologies. This form of trade has pushed the envelope for seafaring and air-based transport technologies and methods all over the world, with amazing flow-on effects of travel, mission, migration, commerce and business. All of these phenomena if conducted in a right and good-hearted way as previously described, have the potential to develop closer working and personal relationships between people of different countries and regions. This can then increase international harmony and peace and ultimately be used to help work toward fairer distribution of wealth between nations globally.

17) Nation trading group - Like minded or different nations trading together for the betterment of each other. Groups of nations working as a trading community. European Union, APEC, ASEAN etc. Bilateral arrangements may still exist within the group countries, but they should not discriminate unfairly compared with the wider group. The unique difference here is that the trading is expanded to benefit all nations instead of just the two preferring each other, often above other trading partners. This should serve to increase the breadth of mutual benefit to all nations in the group and emphasize the aspect of community above self or bilateral interest. The aforementioned principles described in earlier life category entities also apply at this nation- trading level. This model while defining different groups and entities for the purposes of clarity and ease of description, has concluded and in fact proven that the principles and positive characteristics of all elements are thoroughly compatible and consistent, and need to be present in each and flow through to all levels and groupings, in order to be effective and enable *genuine peace* throughout our society. No life category entity can be overlooked or left out. All elements of society are important and play a key role in bringing about *genuine peace*.

18) All-Nation International - A Global collective of nations. This theoretical life category entity describes the bringing together of the government and administrative elements of nations into a combined collective, supposedly for the common good. Whilst this is currently in various stages of implementation at various levels and groupings of nations, and functions within nations, the goal has always been to unite all nations. Its creators I am sure, postulated that it would bring countries closer together and make them easier to administer and govern both locally and internationally. This concept while sounding lofty and beneficial, and for the common good, is also showing signs of serious difficulty, which will require significant modification, or alternatively have to be abandoned altogether. The bottom line is that a world government is just far too large and complex an organization for any single human being, executive committee, or groups of committees to effectively govern and manage as a single entity. This is becoming clear from experience, operation and observation of the early implementations of the European Union. Even the United States of America (USA) is becoming difficult to manage well. It seems obvious to me that smaller, self-governing and self-managing sovereign nations being run as individual nations on a democratic basis, based on Judeo-Christian values, beliefs and worldview, while also working together at the international level for functions which it makes sense to do so, will be the ultimate ideal. A world government would only be a flawed and unmanageable concept and is therefore risky to create, and open to flagrant abuse. This can be seen already where the 'head office' syndrome is becoming evident, in that administrators, legislators, public servants, experts in regulation and red tape, experimental social engineers, and the like are gravitating to the central body and slowly creating an unworkable administrative and socially experimental 'monster' open to abuse by individuals who seek power and influence over people. While the true government and organizational practitioners, the gifted leaders and lovers of people, who have the world's best interest at heart, often remain at the national, state, region or city level and seek to add value to humankind and govern there wisely and well. I know from experience that it is both human and rational behaviour, that whenever one wishes to try to govern or manage something massively large, complex and cumbersome, there needs to be rationalization, standardization, systemization, documentation, digitization, computerization, automation, tighter controls, centralization, constraints on freedoms and ability to act creatively or independently, and the like. As an executive manager of a large global corporation, an engineer, IT specialist, business person, theologian, enlightened apostolic and philosophical leader, consultant and life coach, with skills across a plethora of disciplines I can clearly see that a global world government just will not work. It is therefore dangerous to blindly proceed towards creating such an entity. It would become a bottomless pit of cash consumption, a hive of often futile human activity and bureaucracy, and will just get in the way of true human progress and development, which will occur naturally with good and Godly government at the national level. Nations have been with us since the dawn of civilization and have provided adequate organization at the local level. The ideal model going forward is to standardize aspects which need standardization, for example, decimal currencies, decimal weights and measures, international trading and security standards, English as the global language, etc., and then these progressively strong and healthy nations with good and Godly values will then naturally coalesce and work together as a global federation of nations using these *genuine peace* principles to bring peace to our world. But let's not try to force every nation into one global organization and government. It would struggle under its own weight, rot on the vine and become the greatest abject disaster of all time.

19) An Individual - An individual human being. You may be wondering why I didn't place this life category element at the beginning of the above list, since it is obviously the lowest functional and relational entity in any model describing human behaviour, groupings, boundaries and relationships. Instead, I have as mentioned previously, defined a hierarchy of functional groups, and briefly described their nature, characteristics, similarities, differences, interfaces and need to work together in mature and functional ways in order to move toward any potential state of *genuine peace*. Now, let's explore this individual human life category and the issues, potential, strengths and weaknesses which might affect our personal ability to achieve this objective. After all, everything we aspire to as a society, ultimately comes down to the capability and willingness of each one of us individually and in groups, to acquire the necessary skills, engage in the massive and sustained effort, and make all the necessary selfless sacrifices along the way. Sadly, on the one hand we are the most amazingly creative, intelligent, productive, ingenious, sentient beings with seemingly unlimited potential, yet we can also on occasions, be flawed, weak, greedy, lazy, disinterested, corrupt, self-centred, self-seeking, ambitious or power hungry. This makes the challenge we face in seeking peace as a human race complex and difficult but not impossible... There is much more information on these aspects contained in Chapter 8, and numerous practical solutions and critical success factors are offered.

20) God Himself - The one known by His nature, characteristics and motives, as well as His supportive and directive attributes, to be the One True and Living God. - Many have sought to adequately describe God over the ages. Here are some examples of who He really is:- a) Maker and sustainer of heaven and earth and all things visible and invisible, b) eternal, pre-existent and everlasting, c) present in three forms The Father, The Son (The Lord Jesus Christ) and the Holy Spirit, d) almighty, e) all knowing, f) omni present, g) our provider, h) author and essence of perfect selfless love, i) foundation of our faith, j) source of our hope, k) reason for our joy, l) perfect in nature, m) the engineer of our salvation, n) He enables us to become increasingly like Him in life, and o) the one who positions us to be perfectly sinless beyond death and into eternity. In short, He is the one that is... and makes eminently possible that indescribable state of *genuine peace*.

21) God and Man - this relationship is the model for the first-mentioned husband and wife life category entity and is also pivotal to the achievement of *genuine peace* within, between, and across all life entities. The God-man relationship is entirely unique in creation because it describes a human being's individual, personal, private, personable and confidential relationship with The Divine... Who is the all-knowing, all loving, one and only true and living God. This relationship even exceeds that of a perfectly operating, loving, covenantal relationship between a husband and wife, because one partner in this relationship is already perfect and seated in the heavenly realm, having all the characteristics of God, because He is God. This 'heavenly' relationship should go beyond the bounds of normal human love and friendship, intimacy, oneness and mutuality, which is meant to be present in covenant marriage between a man and a woman. God and mankind are also meant to operate in close and effective team between heaven and earth, to provide for, love, protect and prepare the church i.e., the followers of Jesus, for life and eternity... And out of this miraculous relationship with God also ensues the uniquely designated and required gifting, anointing and authority to lead and nurture the body of Christ family unit, along with all other life category entities and domains of life, in order to provide sound and wise building blocks of society and to help usher in His ultimate and blessed outcome of *genuine peace*. This relationship is the most intricate, intimate, complex, sophisticated, vulnerable, supportive and potentially mutually beneficial of all... exceeding all other types of earthly relationships. God, our Heavenly Father, is the One with which, we will spend the lion's share of time on the journey of life, even exceeding that of one's life partner. Father God will be with us every moment of every day and night. He is interested in every large or small aspect of our daily lives, and even if we were to ignore Him, He will never leave us nor forsake us. It is so worth the effort to work diligently towards the best possible interactions, dialogs and relationship outcomes with Him. Level setting and getting to know and enjoy each other fully and completely, communicating, sharing openly, honestly, understanding, resolving issues, within ourselves personally, and with Him, are pure gold and bring so many benefits mutually and as an individual. Once knowing each other fully, and being fully known, we can work out optimal boundaries and methods of operation, gifting, calling, mission and interest. Some things will be shared together intimately and in quiet retreat, exploring details by way of the Bible and related study, prayer, reflecting, researching, enquiring and listening to the heart of God. There will also be times where we feel like we are operating by ourselves, yet in point of fact, in Spirit, He never leaves our side. At times we may even need to apologize to the Lord for acts of commission or omission which we have come to realize, have been counter to the ideals and goals which He/we are seeking to foster in our lives and the world around us. This allows us to grow individually as well as in concert with Him. The ideal is to achieve a sense of God, and an awareness of His presence and guidance with us, every moment of every day. Achieving *genuine peace* at this level is thoroughly achievable by all, since God is always a willing party seeking our ultimate best good and success. Peace with Father God is also critical to the wellbeing and enjoyment of all individuals, whether in singleness, friendships, marriage, or in life generally. Ultimately, the 'God-man' relationship has the potential to positively benefit the individual, family, church and the whole of humanity. It provides the foundation for every good and worthwhile thing that we human beings can ever do. He truly is the Creator, enabler and sustainer of our wellbeing, creativity and ingenuity... and the only true and reliable source of *genuine peace*. Please join me in seeking to capture the essence and positive principles regarding boundaries, interactions and characteristics of all life category entities described in this chapter, and let's apply all our energy, gifting and calling toward achieving this most precious outcome.

Chapter 6 - Values Enable or Inhibit

Values are social principles, goals, and standards held by an individual, group, class, or society. They are typically the concepts, ideas, norms and objectives which are deemed to have enduring value and worth. The reason they are so important to consider when seeking to engender peace in a social setting, is that values are usually either positive or negative, one might even say right or wrong, and when such values are aspired to and applied in a social setting, they will predispose the group accordingly.

For example, when **negative values** are allowed or encouraged, they lead to un-Godly principles such as; trusting in any other god or no god (idolatry), wilfully creating conflict or unhealthy competition, accepting or encouraging bad relationships, as well as lies, deception, corruption, selfishness, unwillingness to listen and dialog, intransigence, destructive criticism, unfaithfulness, lack of love, un-forgiveness, dishonouring, taking offence, un-thankfulness, lack of respect, impatience, unkindness, unfairness, unreasonableness, violence, lack of self control, propensity toward evil, flawed concepts which don't work, irrational reasoning, unhealthy lifestyles, unsound principles, unachievable goals, poor business acumen, ineffective leadership, not valuing human life, not valuing marriage and family, poor stewardship of resources, lack of generosity, lack of wisdom and foresight, and finally incompetent administration... Now, as I believe you may have already deduced, these will inevitably predispose any group toward negative, often chaotic, destructive and unpredictable social outcomes. Examples of such **negative values** which would lead to the above are:-

We value:-
- Not having to revere any god, we worship only human endeavour (idolatry)
- Not accepting any outside influence or direction (rebellion)
- Not accepting any starting point or guidelines for self conduct (pride)
- Inventing our own social norms and deciding what's right and wrong
- Delighting in conflict, and purposefully creating adversarial situations
- Not bothering to resolve broken human relationships, letting them fester
- Telling lies and creating deception whenever and wherever we choose
- Always putting our own selfish agenda above others
- Not listening, dialoguing or negotiating unless it serves our own goals
- Choosing to criticize and mock whatever, whomever, whenever we like
- Making only loose, transitory alliances in order to achieve our own ends
- Not honouring or respecting anyone, taking 'offence' whenever we choose
- Providing poor, inconsistent, irrational leadership and direction
- Refusing to set reasonable and rational work goals and deadlines

- Never forgiving others, and holding grudges indefinitely and at whim
- Not accepting any moral or social construct as being positive or the norm
- Redefining societal norms on the latest or most base experimental ideas
- Including ideas from wicked sources without any filters or forethought
- Allowing noisy minorities and radical agendas to drive our way of life
- Structuring our governments on civic compliance rather public service
- Applying whatever force we need to in order to govern the ensuing chaos

Now I acknowledge that we don't all operate with all of these negative values. However, we are no longer teaching our youth a consistent set of sound values, or positive ways of living, in our schools or other learning institutions. This means that there is therefore an increasing propensity toward this negative direction, which if not corrected or contained, would allow our society to deteriorate until these types of behaviour became the norm. This would lead to increasing chaos and heartache, as well as even less desirable and often untenable ways of life.

On the other hand, the opposites of these more base values will typically be **positive**, and if applied seriously will help to create a more natural, workable and desirable order, tending toward peace, hope, effectiveness, productivity and love.

Examples of such positive values are:-

We value:-
- Revering the One True and Living God who created and sustains all things and always has our best interest at heart
- Having a rich and accurate set of timeless guidelines for life conduct
- Being given an effective set of social norms, rights and wrongs
- Delighting in peace, and purposefully choosing to be makers of peace
- Having the tools and methods to heal broken hearts and relationships
- Always telling the truth and operating openly and transparently
- Considering our own goals within the context of God's bigger picture
- Listening, dialoguing and negotiating in a wise, just, fair and rational way
- Objective, uplifting, constructive criticism without mocking or vilifying
- Strong, enduring alliances with like-minded people to better the world
- Pursuit of positive wisdom for life as a determined goal
- Honouring and valuing everyone with wise boundaries and taking no offence
- Providing clear, wise, consistent, rational Godly leadership and direction
- Reasonable and rational work goals and deadlines toward good outcomes
- Always forgiving others, with wise boundaries and not holding grudges
- Applying the predefined tried, proven social norms given to us from the beginning

- That government should serve the good of the people not the reverse
- Use positive values which predispose toward an orderly well-behaved society
- When change is necessary, to accommodate a new technology etc. the changes are made within the above positive guidelines and values.

These positive values really do make a difference and provide a sound base on which to build a mature, developing society, with all its basic elements potentially operating at peace. This kind of society will naturally improve for the better day by day as more and more people choose to live by these values and thereby gain the support, blessing and positive outcomes which God promises as a result of living this way.

Let's now proceed to test the characteristics which I distilled earlier as being germane to achieving *genuine peace* and articulate some positive values and related goals and actions which would naturally and logically be required in order to lead to and support those requirements.

Characteristics of *genuine peace* and some related values:-

1) Feeling safe, secure, settled and protected - a) These very necessary aspects of *genuine peace* will always require a common set of Judeo-Christian values to drive the day to day operations, laws and practices in all domains of society b) Such values encourage and support genuinely and commonly accepted good, gracious, compassionate, peaceful, respectful, just and wise behaviour of all citizens c) Security agencies, police, army, air force and public servants are also to be governed by these values. d) Freedom of speech, gathering and association are valued, allowed and encouraged for all. e) Human life, marriage, sexual fidelity, pregnancy, birth, motherhood, fatherhood, children, family, homes, neighbourhoods, communities, suburbs, cities, states, nations, vocations, personal assets, property-title and ownership are all valued, accepted as basic building blocks of the healthy society, and are fully protected and enabled in law and in common accepted practice.

2) Having a sense of being provided for, nurtured, succoured and faring well - a) Productive work is highly valued in society and all are encouraged to be actively engaged. b) Every citizen is encouraged to obtain an education, based on the above values, which would lead to a chosen values-based vocation. c) Where some are not able to fulfill the requirements of a typical standard vocation, other assisted or supported occupations suited to the individual's capability will ideally be provided. d) Reasonable, affordable, sustainable welfare safety-net will be provided, wherever individuals are not able to work at all. e) Individuals and siblings who for whatever reason do not have access to family support will ideally be provided with access to values based family and social support by way of friendship, mentoring, community housing, fostering or adoption on a needs and availability basis. f) Healthy lifestyles which enhance rather than detract from peace are encouraged. g) A variety of positive community and charity organizations of diverse types will be fostered and encouraged to cover all the values-based needs and interests of the society. h) And finally healthy, balanced, wholesome, uplifting, bible-based, life-applying, Judeo-Christian churches will be encouraged to flourish and proliferate everywhere, and will provide and nurture the under-girding faith and values system of society. i) Finally, those hopefully small and decreasing numbers of people who choose lifestyles which predispose against *genuine peace* and wholesome relationships, and encourage the likes of violence, crime, strife, terror, drug abuse, occult practice, demonic practices and so forth will receive the punishments, constraints, confinements and reparations of a righteous and fair legal system. The system would be designed to seek to protect the peaceful public, keep troublemakers off the streets indefinitely if necessary, and give opportunity for rehabilitation and restoration only when serious attempts are made to do so.

3) Being debt-free, unencumbered, - a) Proper values based financial-management, life, business and legal skills will be taught from an early age in school, family, church, and other community organizations. b) People will be encouraged to be generous and yet live within their means, and to understand how life and business transactions operate, and financial and legal commitments are made, consciously or unwittingly. c) Individuals and families would ideally borrow only to buy assets which will appreciate in value, and only from reputable agents and lenders, making sure not to over commit, and risk loan failure or bankruptcy. d) Compulsory retirement saving will be encouraged directly from salary and business profits, with a view toward self-funding for the majority of citizens, when one's paid vocation has come to an end. e) Additional personal savings over and above compulsory retirement funds will also be encouraged.

4) Having no stress, worry, anxiety - a) Focusing on a sound and committed relationship with the One True and Living God, and living by His principles and values, reduces most life anxiety levels, and they can actually be radically minimized or even eradicated in many life situations. b) He says if we feel anxious about anything we can pray and ask him in an attitude of humility and willingness to take His advice, and as we move in the way He instructs, the peace of God, which transcends understanding, will guide us and guard our hearts and minds. c) Reading, reflecting and bringing appropriate life application from a small section of the Bible every day, will help to develop the above disciplines, in a broader and deeper fashion. And this will also guide us to maintain good motives, attitudes, habits and behaviours, which will ultimately lead us to this beautiful place of peace. d) We also need to be conscious of God's perfect timing and be patient and willing to rest in Him, trusting Him as our Lord and Teacher, learning what we are meant to in each challenging life situation, then being ready to move forward into the next step, as and when instructed. e) Being confident in faith that no matter what 'life' throws at us, whether big, small, offensive, hurtful, painful, rejecting, rude, arrogant, thoughtless, ill-conceived or illogical we can trust in Him to see us through. And when people are hard hearted, resentful, bitter, cruel or traumatizing toward us, whether in truth or in error, that we can know for sure that In Christ we can always have the victory, if we are prepared to work through any necessary process or pain and seek to fully resolve and settle the issues. f) Knowing always that He has gone before us and prepared the way, and will guide us, even through the valleys of darkness and on toward the Light of The Lord Jesus Christ and ultimately good outcomes.

5) Being in good relationship with others - a) Firstly we need to believe wholeheartedly that good healthy sound relationships are important to a cohesive, workable enjoyable society. I believe this is self-evident, yet I am aware that many philosophies either cannot or will not seek to engender wholesome win-win relationships across society. Some even work to the destruction of healthy relationships by seeking to implement hierarchies of class or control, powerful ruling elites, 'us and them', winners and losers, and the like. Such approaches ultimately bring chaos as those who are being 'hard done by' inevitably rise up to take things into their own hands. b) Then it's important to be prepared to selflessly, purposefully and tirelessly, invest the time, effort, resources, energy, prayer, commitment, determination and enthusiasm toward achieving a philosophy and strategy of strong, healthy, relationships in all the elements and domains of society in which we operate or have influence. This will sometimes require us to believe in what seems impossible at the time, because our society is really struggling in that particular area, or worse still seems to be actually strongly working against sound relationships. However, I assure you, with God, all things are possible especially when we are working on

His agendas. c) Finally, it also must be noted that at times we will need to resist the individuals and spiritual forces which are actually often ruthlessly working against sound relationships. Sometimes they are entrenched and endemic even in very powerful positions. This requires fortitude, courage, and serious dedication to listen to God for specific instructions, as well as a willingness to work individually and with other like-minded people toward agreed plans to bring about positive change.

6) Having a sense of hope, joy and happiness - a) Hope is a mandatory requirement for healthy individuals and societies. If one truly believes there is no hope, there is really nothing to live for, nothing worth working toward and it leads to the concept of 'eat drink and be merry for tomorrow we die'. This is extremely unhealthy, and I have seen the detrimental effect firsthand in a country which was occupied by communism for a generation. b) The only true source of hope in this universe is in the One True and Living God. Flesh and blood or other gods and spirits cannot provide credible, eternal, strong and reliable hope because they have only limited, finite, flawed, unreliable, constrained capability to do so, and are always working to their own selfish agendas, which are typically contrary to the wellbeing of humankind. c) And hope does not travel alone. In order to experience true hope, one also needs to experience the fullness of faith and love. Faith to believe Jesus died for our sin and to receive and live by that knowledge, as well as faith to believe that in Christ Jesus things can and will get better, as we journey with Him and do as he asks us to do. Then finally, there is love. Agape love, the power to create a wonderful world, which is the subject of my third book Learning Places: *Real Love* and is one of the main supernatural agents for bringing peace into the world. It gives power to overcome darkness by desiring the uttermost best good for all and doing and praying all that is necessary to make it happen through the agency and power of Heaven. d) True joy and happiness can then flow naturally from well-founded faith, hope, and loving and being loved, within this supernatural agency and canopy of agape. And this process ultimately leads to abundant life, which is being truly, fully and selflessly loved by God and some of His key men and women in our life, while also seeking to live out our lives within the most wonderful, complete, satisfying, perfect will and purpose of God. Then, while being able to love others with this world changing love... whether they respond initially or not... and also personally and corporately experiencing the power of its effectiveness in our own lives, we will begin to experience a pure unadulterated joy and deeply profound happiness, which is utterly exhilarating, satisfying and difficult to describe.

7) Having faith that all things will ultimately work together for good - a) This is a powerful promise of God which I have found to be utterly true and reliable and seen at work a myriad of times in my life and that of other faithful followers of the Lord Jesus Christ. It cannot be claimed and experienced by just any person on earth, but for all those who love God and are called according to His purpose, it is a miraculous and wonderful reality. That is, unless we allow it to be stolen away by negative, critical, destructive thinking, mindsets and self-talk, or if we are walking in disobedience to our calling in Him. It means that even if things feel 'bad' or look like setbacks, suffering or persecution at the time, the ultimate outcome will eventually bring good into our lives and/or the circumstances of those around us. This promise and its related process, when entered into fully will manifest the truth that suffering will bring perseverance, and perseverance character, and character hope... a hope which cannot be disappointed because it is backed by all the power and promise of Heaven.

8) Being blessed, favoured and preferred - a) This is similar in that there are many promises to those sons and daughters of God who have found peace with Him, who serve King Jesus wholeheartedly, and are passionately and obediently involved in His cause to redeem the world. The banner and resources of God, including the hosts of heaven, guide and protect these ones because He loves them and because they are critically and importantly engaged in His campaign to bring in the Kingdom of God.

9) Being in good health and wellbeing in body, soul and spirit - a) In order to be truly at peace, one must achieve an adequate level of health and wellbeing in body, soul and spirit. This includes the mind, will and emotions, our physical body, as well as the human spirit and its relationship with God's Holy Spirit. Further and more comprehensive information related to this topic is provided in Chapter 8.

10) Having a sense of prospering, flourishing and succeeding - a) There are many values and principles in the Bible which, when lived out consistently in our lives, will reinforce and bring substance to this blessing and others like it, which are key and necessary characteristics of feeling truly at peace. It's difficult to feel peaceful in life, and in our heart, when everything we try seems to fail. This should not be the norm. Yes, there will be apparent 'failures' along the way, but they should and will be occurring within the greater framework of general success, if one is walking in tune with the values framework and specific will of God. b) The books of Proverbs and Psalms are replete with principles and promises which cover this area. They are well worth a read, along with practical application in daily life. You will notice an immediate difference if you've never tried to live by them before. c) Some examples in addition to those mentioned above are, honour the Lord with your substance and the first fruit of your increase, and your barns will be filled with plenty and your presses burst with new wine. d) Find true Godly wisdom and you shall walk safely and not stumble. e) Don't give guarantee for another person's debt. This gives the other person and their related parties and circumstances the ability to damage, disrupt even ruin your financial position. f) Be a person of your word. Don't promise anything rashly, without appropriate, wise, forethought and prayer. But having agreed to do something, always seek to fulfill your promises or alternatively explain justly, graciously, fairly and righteously why you cannot. g) Maintain a close working relationship and friendship with God, always living by His principles and commandments and doing what is right in His eyes. This way of living in relation to God and humankind will tend us toward maximum favour and ultimately peace.

11) Feeling that anything which has been lost will ultimately be restored - a) There are many promises in this area as well. They usually require as above a healthy, sustained and wholesome, committed relationship with God, both generally and particularly. And usually promise return of that which is lost in this life and/or in the next, often with interest and manifold increase and multiplication. We need to constantly walk in this promise by faith, with thankfulness, even when circumstances seem to be working against us. God is our ultimate benefactor, and He will not be mocked!

12) That your borders are secure and vital places robust and intact - a) This promise is stated in many ways throughout the Bible and applies to faithful and dedicated followers of God, who are unwilling to compromise on His principles, values and way of life. They apply to individuals, families, communities, cities and nations and are a key part of the heart cry and basic need of every human being. If we are committed to serving, listening to God and doing what He says, all the resources of Heaven plus anointed wisdom here on earth, will be available to understand how we should conduct ourselves, to protect our borders, as well as both our personal and corporate innermost entities, assets and values. Sometimes, this will require firm, forceful, protective and decisive action, and on other occasions a gentle, more tender thoughtful, negotiable approach.

13) A knowing that your internal resources are intact and in good supply - a) Comments apply as above, as well as. b) Promises like 'God shall supply all your needs according to His riches in glory'. c) 'Ours is not a spirit of fear but of power and of love and of a sound mind'. Once again, we need to walk in faith to see the promised result, and always in God's perfect timing. On occasions, we have to suffer, work and endure patiently, in order to achieve an outcome, much like soldiers on the front line of a battlefield.

14) That external supplies are abundantly available when needed - a) He wonderfully promises that as long as we do not begin to give our allegiance to other gods and idols, he will continue to 'give us this day our daily bread'. b) And 'feed us like he does the sparrows, the grass and flowers of the field'. c) 'That the sun will shine each day and the moon by night'. d) And 'one season will consistently follow another and rain, seedtime and harvest will always be available to His faithful'. These are promises we are given and need to internalize and live by, in order to guide our journey of life on His way toward *genuine peace*.

15) Being certain that you can deliver on any reasonable assignment which you are asked to accomplish - a) This is true because of abovementioned provisions, values and promises and knowing that we can do all things through Christ who strengthens us. b) That there is nothing new under the sun, that all good ideas and perfect gifts come down by revelation from above c) That He will always make a way for us to do that which we are destined to do. d) And providing we are always seeking to walk and live obediently within His perfect will and purpose for our lives.

16) Knowing that you can recover from any past problems which may have occurred - a) He is the God of the second chance, and third and fourth and so on. b) In Him we have access to salvation, healing, miracles, a sound mind, healing of memories and broken hearts, redemption, justification, reconciliation, restoration, sanctification and glorification. c) Nothing is too hard for God when we stand in right relationship with Him and walk and work through the issues as He leads.

17) That any loss can be recovered from - Refer to items 11) to 16) above.

18) That we have access to earthly and heavenly wisdom for life - They who lack wisdom can ask and it will be given without reserve.

19) Having a healthy sense of giving and receiving - a) A generous at heart, and wise and disciplined steward, will always have sufficient to give and to do that which God asks. We should always give as the Lord guides us to with joy and gladness of heart, remembering that sometimes provision only begins to come when we first step out in obedience to the will of God.

20) Being complete, full, satisfied, whole, lacking nothing - The combined effect of all of the above.

21) Able to maintain a place or attitude of solitude, quietness and rest in the midst of any challenge - a) The combined effect of all of the above, and those below make this possible... This is the place where *genuine peace* can flourish and give strength and stability to our lives and our world. b) Together with knowing that God himself and all the host of heaven are on our side, leading, guiding, protecting, nurturing, providing, encouraging and mentoring, with the perfect and capable intention of helping us to succeed in this life, make this world a better place, and be prepared for eternity. This is the heart of why we are here on this earth.

22) Being in a multifaceted State of ONE-ness - The combined effect and outcome of all of the above, and those below. ONE-ness is an expression I have used which seeks to capture the fullness of what it means to be in a perfect state of *genuine peace*. I have endeavoured to fully describe the concept by breaking it down into smaller practical elements below and defining each one individually. This ONE-ness should not be confused with the new age or science fiction/fantasy concepts which are typically more passive than active in state and process.

23) One with God - a) This state embodies knowing who God is, in all His fullness, beauty, power, perfection and wonder and having a strong, enduring, open, honest, committed, dedicated, transparent, vulnerable, humble, respectful, obedient, honouring and loving relationship with Him. b) We also know, value and relate to Him as Lord, creator, saviour, redeemer, restorer, sanctifier, reconciler, sustainer, provider, protector, nurturer, father, mother, champion, sponsor, mentor and guide. c) We enter into the fullness of the wonderful relationship which He has made available to us in Christ Jesus and experience first-hand the depth, beauty and reality of the meaning of all the above. For example, we put God first in every aspect of our lives because He knows best. We see our world accurately and clearly by looking at it through His heavenly worldview. We don't pretend we can have secrets from God, and we share everything with Him. Trust Him fully with our innermost thoughts, loving no other more than we love Him, always seeking His perfect wisdom and guidance, and having a respectful attitude that He is the boss, and a passionate willingness to obey His voice in our lives. d) And finally, we need to connect with Him fully and maturely with appropriate boundaries and an attitude of surrender, love and trust, in all of the roles He so generously makes himself available to us, in this life and the next, as described in 23 above. Examples are as follows. As The Lord, He is sovereign and not limited in any way, having absolute authority to do as He pleases within the confines of His perfect nature. He administers justice to all, giving us all that we deserve, with the exception of those who are in Christ and who, through His sacrifice on the cross, can obtain mercy as we walk in obedience. In order to have peace with and be at one with God we have to take advantage of what Jesus offers us through His death and resurrection. There is no other way. The price for sin has been paid. Considered in our own right we are all sinners, we cannot even pay the price of our own sin, and it is said that the wages of sin are death. This is because when we die in this life our spirit cannot enter into heaven unless it has been made sinless through Christ. There cannot be any sin in heaven. Therefore, unredeemed souls go to another place which has been reserved for the demons who are also hopeless sinners.

This may sound strange to some of my readers, yet it is a very serious truth and reality which one has to address in this life. What will we do with Jesus? Will we reject His life saving and life changing loving generous offer, and reject Him and heaven as well, thus facing the hopelessness of an eternity without Christ's redemption. Or will we whole heartedly accept His loving offer, say we are sorry for our sin and all offences we have committed toward Him and others, receive His gift of redemption, invite him into our lives and begin to walk in newness of life? This is called being 'born again'. This single act of humility and obedience will change us forever in this life and in eternity. The result of this act of faith and acceptance is receiving of the Holy Spirit and nature of God into our hearts, so we can appropriate this amazing redemption, and have the potential ability to walk through life in a Christ-like manner, full of the power of His Holy Spirit, living and doing as Jesus would do. He will also give us access to a heavenly language which is designed for us to talk personally with him when not using our own language. It is called tongues and gives us the ability to pray when we cannot or don't wish to use our own native language. We can then also experience the fullness and openness of a personal relationship and friendship with God, which is not possible while sin is separating us from Him and giving the devil free reign in our lives. Knowing Him personally and intimately we can then develop a relationship where He will share His heart with us, answer our questions, teach and train us, and unfold mysteries and unknowns. He can also help us deal with a myriad of personal issues. ONE-ness with the One True and Living God is such a wonderful idyllic place to live. Further information on this topic is contained in Chapter 8.

24) One with humankind - a) Human beings are not meant to be alone. In our natural state we value and seek out relationship, family and community. To feel at one, we need to have positive relationships with others. b) It takes significant experience, knowledge, time, effort and emotion to build strong healthy relationships, and this is a really important life skill to develop. Chapter 4 contains significant information on this topic. c) In addition to what has already been mentioned it should be noted that childhood and family experiences are the best learning places for acquiring these skills. Ideally building healthy relationships is something we should all be able to learn while growing up in our family homes. Where possible, we need to keep our natural families strong, functional and healthy in order to improve quality of relationships in our society. Where family complexities occur, we need to apply the principles espoused in this book to make the best we can of each situation. It is nevertheless not appropriate or possible for schools to achieve this goal well, because they need to be focused on teaching basic reading, writing and arithmetic type skills, not be focusing on social values and lifestyles and such. I should also say that it is extremely difficult for the state, other institutions or any fabricated imitation of family to fulfill the need which we all have to belong to a natural family and relate to other life category entities. This requires positive Judeo-Christian values to be in pervasive operation, in order to have a reasonable chance of helping ourselves and others to achieve this desirable, idyllic and needful type of one-ness. These values must again become mainstream in order to achieve *genuine peace*.

25) One with self - a) In order to achieve or at least approach an ideal state of peace and ONE-ness within ourselves, we need to be free from any negative spiritual or practical impacts which we may have inherited due to the actions or inactions of our forefathers. b) Our internal values and belief systems need to be aligned with that which is right, good, honourable and true, as well as being as close as possible to the values, beliefs and worldview of the purest biblical form of Judeo-Christianity. c) It is also important that any inner emotional, physical, mental, social, spiritual or psychological damage, which may have occurred during our existence on this earth, whether by hurt, confusion or misunderstanding is all healed, reoriented and resolved as well. And finally, we need d) deliverance, together with healing, re-orientation and resolution as in 25 c) above, as well as freedom, and protection from the oppression of external spiritual entities, whether that be by way of direct or indirect means. e) There is no fixed sequence to this process. One can start with 25 a) but then 25 b), and d) typically need to be worked on as an interdependent group, usually by focusing gently and with consistent prayer, reflection, common sense and the Lord Jesus' leading and timing, dealing first with an overall approach, as in prayer and declaration using the likes of **Isaiah 61:1, 'The Spirit of The Lord God is upon me; because He has anointed me to preach good tidings unto the meek; He hath sent me to bind up the broken hearted; to proclaim liberty to the captives, and the opening of prison to them that are**

bound'. The Lord will often do a sovereign healing, restorative miracle at the declaration of His word in this way... then one can focus on residual issues and aspects on a needs basis. Further information on this topic is provided in Chapters 7 and 8.

26) One with spouse - a) Much has been said previously on this topic. Husband and wife one- ness is unique in the earth and is meant to be the deepest most fulfilling relationship one can have here in this life. b) The principles of section 24)- One with Humankind also apply here but a married couple are designed to enjoy a much deeper, even more loving and intimate relationship than with other fellow human beings. c) And the concepts described in 23)-One with God apply as well, in that earthly marriage is a temporal example of how our relationship with God is meant to be. Except that our relationship with each other as husband and wife is as equals, mutually accountable before God. d) Section 25)-One with self is deeply relevant too, in that unless we achieve a high level of one-ness ourselves we will struggle to achieve the very best that we can as a married couple. e) The next level of achieving one-ness in a married couple relationship depends heavily on the quality, effectiveness, enjoyment and intimacy of communication and conversation. f) Consistency of spiritual beliefs are important in achieving one-ness, and as mentioned before need to be based upon the model of spirituality, which is trustworthy, true and actually works. g) Complementary and compatible character traits are important and flow naturally from spiritual beliefs, if those beliefs are viable and worthy, and consistent with one's partner. h) The way we manage our finances needs to be fiscally sound and consistent between partners, even if that means encouraging the one with the stronger more effective management skills to take the lead. i) Conflict management skills need to be mature, effective and compatible and always seek to identify and ultimately resolve foundational issues and root causes. j) How we enjoy spending our leisure is also ideal when it is consistent and complementary. This can however always be balanced, negotiated and compromised where there are practical and reasonable issues why one cannot enjoy their spouse's ideas of leisure. k) Compatibility of husband and wife's networks of friends adds to relationship one-ness and enjoyment, yet there is always room for dialog and compromise in this area as well. 1) Understanding and being comfortable with each other's personal style and habits affects levels of intimacy and harmony. Sometimes we will ideally need to change what could be deemed 'bad', 'anti-social', hurtful, offensive or illegal habits, and it is in the interest of enhancing oneness, if we are willing to listen, negotiate and compromise with our spouse in these areas. Then finally and extremely importantly, there is m) sexual intimacy which is of foundational and pivotal importance to husband and wife one-ness. Mutual availability, enjoyment, adoration, love, respect, tenderness, gentleness, kindness, patience, thoughtfulness, consideration, and a willingness to learn from each other that which we find most satisfying, together with an attitude of selflessness, and having the desire to please our spouses above ourselves, are all critical to achieving one-ness in this area. In conclusion, each one of these categories is important in its own right, but when all are applied, in a positive, complementary, comprehensive and consistent way across the whole relationship, it will bring high quality one-ness outcomes and significantly increase couple enjoyment. My third book Learning Places: Real Love also provides further substantial information on these topics.

27) One with family - a) One-ness in family flows firstly from one-ness with God, ideally for both husband and wife and the children. If the couple can also achieve one-ness with each other, then this provides the very best and only foundation upon which family one-ness can be fully achieved. Nevertheless, even if not all family members have achieved one-ness, there are extremely positive effects if even one member begins to explore and ultimately achieve a modicum of one-ness. Initially it can cause some turmoil, but one-ness is extremely compelling and practically and relationally contagious, it will soon begin to have positive effect on the whole family. b) Another key element is that the children should honour their mother and father. This comes with a great blessing upon the child firstly, then the parent and then the whole family. Honouring does not mean one has to agree with everything the person says, or blindly obey their instructions, but it is possible to value the person and relate respectfully with them, even love them, but this should always be within appropriate values and boundaries. A wise, loving parent will always seek to be a good role model and provide sound, age-appropriate direction, and fair discipline, along with a place for dialog, where the children can interpret, learn, understand and ideally ask questions for clarity as well as negotiate outcomes. c) The principles of one-ness with self and humankind also apply to family one-ness. d) Great effort and intention should be consistently, fairly and lovingly applied, within the family unit, to particularly and positively nurture and develop the self of our children, and not stunt, abuse, neglect or damage them in any way. The family is the ultimate and ideal place to build the one-ness of each new generation, and this will increase the one-ness across society.

28) One with friends -a) The majority of principles and values mentioned in 27) - One with family, also apply to friends. And b) healthy groups of friends should ideally have access to good sound mother and father role models, particularly for the younger ones. c) Positive groups of friends can also help compensate for the lack of healthy host families, where this is not practically available to growing children and youth in their own blood families. d) In fact, the key elements of all the above sections will also apply in principle to friends, with the exception of sexual intimacy between husband and wife. This I have found on the journey of life, cannot be applied outside of the domain of marriage, without disturbing or damaging one-ness quite seriously in one way or another, both between the individuals involved and all other parties which are affected directly or indirectly, including society in general.

29) One with acquaintances - a) One-ness with acquaintances also embodies the principles and values of 28) One with friends above. b) The difference here is that acquaintances are pre- friendship and therefore more loose-knit and tentative. They are still getting to know each other, enquiring, dialoguing, communicating, connecting at various levels, and still building and earning trust one with another, endeavouring to decide whether they could or should be friends, or just remain acquaintances. c) Even if people do not become friends, there should always be a goal of maintaining congenial and positive acquaintance and fellowship. When such a relationship does not yet appear possible, in the interest of enhancing *genuine peace* at the community, city or national level, one should always persist with relational follow-through described in Chapter 4, until such time as the issues involved are resolved and a sound relationship begins to become possible. We rarely invest adequate time in this area. Like speed dating, we often just briefly connect, make preliminary observations, feel 'vibes', make judgments instead of discernments, and swiftly come to conclusions, sometimes accurate and sometimes otherwise. This behaviour of not taking the time and emotional effort to connect properly and fairly, and then ignoring, avoiding or even ostracizing people, creates massive social problems in society and inhibits and reduces our one-ness and *genuine peace*. Even if we find serious reasons why resolution of relationship issues is not possible, there is always more which can be done to identify and resolve the underlying problems. This may be at the individual specific relationship level, or it may be a broader community or society-wide issue. Sometimes, it can be inappropriate laws, regulations, conventions, rules, written or unwritten, ideas, behaviours, cultural or religious practice, and philosophical concepts etc which need to change in order to progress toward *genuine peace*. But as long as we can stick to the facts, speak truth, carefully, openly, honestly, transparently and fairly... observe what is working in society and what is not... and be open to dialog regarding necessary change, there will always be hope that these types of issues can be resolved.

30) One with workmates - a) 29) One with acquaintances' principles and values also generally apply in the workplace. b) In workplaces however the bosses or owners can by their very behaviour and expectations either enhance or reduce one-ness in their offices and in the wider community. And since they usually take or are given opportunity to direct and govern group behaviour, they have an inordinate influence on one-ness. Common sense would say however that the principles and values espoused here for individuals, must also apply to bosses without bias. In the same way individuals must be able to call each other and their bosses to account when behaviour is the opposite of that which will bring one-ness and *genuine peace*.

31) One with enemies - a) Agape love when applied with wisdom, compassion, strategic intent and the guidance and anointing of God, can melt the heart of the hardest, most aggressive of enemies, stopping them dead in their tracks, and speaking directly into their spirit, the things of God. This will often neutralize their negative intentions, bring them to their knees, and give them every chance to have a change of heart, while positioning them to receive healing and new life from the Lord. Even if this does not happen immediately, it will sow the seeds of something powerful into their heart for possible later positive engagement. b) It is important to note nevertheless, that some people just don't want relationship or seem incapable of developing friendships. It is a two-way street. Those who are trying to build bridges may therefore feel stressed when it doesn't work out. Our responsibility before God is simply to as far as it depends upon us, seek to be at peace with all people, manage the disappointment with appropriate boundaries, positive mental discipline and prayer, in order to protect our hearts from damage and seek to keep the door open for the possibility of change in the future. Some people also persist in doing all sorts of evil and inappropriate activities and this makes connection even more problematic without becoming embroiled in the sin and immoral or criminal behaviours, because light will not mix with darkness. Great patience, longsuffering, wisdom and a magnanimous Godly compassion are required in order to persevere in such cases, but God is a miracle working God. Please refer to my third book Learning Places: Real Love for further extensive information on this topic.

32) One with the earth - a) Our earth has been created and is being sustained in such beautiful systematic balance and working order and could not have happened by chance. This is to be honoured and preserved in the interest of us all. b) Sadly though, many have become obsessed with minutiae, related to preservation of the earth and often focus on issues which are untrue, unfounded, hypothetical, un-provable and purely speculative. I am also convinced artificial crises are even invented to create the impression that the world is at risk and allow certain governments to levy taxes and implement laws, red tape and controls in order to achieve other ends. For example, carbon pollution was an entire fallacy and prefabrication. Carbon and carbon dioxide are naturally occurring and catered for routinely by various elements of nature. Carbon dioxide which is exuded through breathing is continually being converted, reabsorbed and converted back to carbon and oxygen by plants and trees. Another was global warming. How can we possibly make such radical inferences from no more than 100 years of data? It really is unbelievable! And yet it was pushed with such brash confidence, by so many supposedly learned people that many were afraid to contest it for fear of being vilified. On the basis of global warming theory, the cost of energy has been forcefully and radically increased by ill-founded targets, taxes and incentives. This has precipitated actions prematurely, which would have happened naturally, as the cost of alternative energies became reduced by technical advance. Examples are the radically early closures of viable coal-fired power stations and unwillingness to build new clean versions. Water quality scare tactics have happened as well. These were brought about by technology now being able to see and count bacteria where previously we could only guess. Another is the refusal to build dams which has now created water shortages. All of these have been used to levy higher taxes and increase utility prices to customers, build ridiculously expensive desalination plants etc, and there seems to be no end to this profligacy. c) Nevertheless, we should have plans for rational care of our planet. For example, stopping deforestation and generally increasing planting of trees with wise harvesting and replacement. d) Caution should be applied with technologies and approaches which can potentially pollute or unduly deplete our underground water tables, like poorly designed septic tanks and inappropriate chemical drilling. e) Improving efficiency of cars. f) Reduction of harmful chemicals in building materials. g) Limiting or eliminating extrusion of toxic waste into the air, rivers and oceans. This type of rational protection of the earth is good, sound, logical and beneficial to all. And does not create exorbitant taxing and controls. This type of conservation or sustainability generally makes the world better because it makes sense, does not create winners and losers and increases harmony in community and with our wonderful planet.

33) One with creatures - a) The creatures which have been made and proliferate upon our beautiful earth are marvellous in their wonder, variety, harmony and interdependence. b) Creatures exist in the air, on and under the earth and in the oceans and abound by the billions. Every creature seems to have a purpose and amazing synergy with its environment and other creatures. Not one has been newly created since the beginning, all have been with us from the start. c) It is right and proper for us to understand more and more about what God has created, together with their amazing capabilities. Many human 'inventions' have been inspired by what we see in creation and copied or extended. d) We should also seek to ensure, where possible and appropriate, that our species are not disappearing haphazardly and wastefully from the earth. e) We should not however use an endangered creature to seek to stop an already started multi-billion-dollar project created for the betterment of humankind. It's better to explore environmental impacts before starting and weigh up any issues against the value to humanity of the planned project. f) We should seek not to unnecessarily destroy creature habitats as we humans expand upon the earth. g) Animals, birds and fish however should not be given more value than human beings. These creatures were created for the feeding, service and enjoyment of humans, and while we should maintain and treat them kindly, we should not idolize them unduly. h) And yes, it is acceptable to harvest fully mature, dead or dying trees from the forest for use for other purposes. i) And finally, private or commercial farming of creatures for food and services are also acceptable if done justly, humanely and with a high level of sustainability.

34) One with plants - a) Principles and values described in 33) One with creatures above, also apply in concept to this category. b) In addition, it should be noted that plants are the most amazing and seemingly unending food supply for humankind. Once there was a ridiculous statement that the planet could only cater for about three billion humans, but we are currently and easily catering for populations of far more than twice that number. Plants are by far the greatest and most successful and prolific food supply of all, and we continue to find more ways to use them, including the plants of the sea. c) Plants also contain medicines and natural remedies for many of the maladies of humankind. d) Harmony, synergy and productivity with plants are critical to the success, longevity and peacefulness of humankind and will continue to be so.

We do well to continue to invest in research and innovations in this area.

35) One with the 'Universe' i.e., with the will, timing and direction of God - a) The One True and Living God and the fulfillment of His overall plan and timeline, are of paramount importance to the destiny of the universe and in achieving *genuine peace*. In fact, it is fair to say that *genuine peace* actually begins to occur as we wilfully, successfully and joyfully fall into line with God's perfect plans. It is both a signpost and a reward. **He is Creator and sustainer of all that is, and He has a perfect plan for all of humanity**, which includes seeking after our highest best good, both personally and collectively. Because of who He is, what He's capable of, and the critical importance of His campaign, it does not pay to be at cross purposes with Him. We have been given free will, so that we are not the equivalent of robots, but our free will as I've said, ideally needs to fall within the bounds of God's higher purposes. His ways are higher than our ways, and where our individual or collective free will and choices would negate some important higher strategic objective, The Lord must do something in order to make sure that His purpose is or can still be achieved. Examples of such Divine intervention would typically be a miracle breakthrough on an impossible battlefront during a military campaign, a man jumping out of an airplane without a parachute and living, someone rising from the dead, a suicide attempt being thwarted, angelic visitation stopping or enabling something important, a 'natural' disaster which affects someone or a group of people's circumstances in ways that change history, and so on. **This also applies regarding**

purpose. God has a destiny for our lives which is usually critically important to achieve, yet it is meant to bring great joy, adventure, fulfillment, learning and a myriad of other things into our life, as well as a sense of being part of a higher mosaic of meaning for humankind. A kingdom mosaic if you like. If we don't seek out these purposes and fulfill them, not only will we have reduced enjoyment, even a sense of frustration in life, but God will also have to arrange another person to do what He really wanted us to do. I don't know how you feel about this, but I certainly don't want to fall short of God's very best purposes for my life. An example of this for me was when I married my amazing, second wife, Kathy almost eight years after my wonderful, first wife Junie had tragically died at the young age of fifty-six. Decisions like this are massive and affect almost every part of one's life but having come to the realization in my seventh year of being single that I was in fact meant to re-marry, and to whom I was to be married, it was the obvious and most sensible choice for us to make. Marrying my second wife, Kathy, has proven to be one of the best decisions of my entire life, and I just know in my spirit, it was part of God's perfect plan. In fact, I have come to realize that He already knew about our second marriage long before the creation of the World. Amazing, isn't it? And even though both our lives are now more complex, they are also much more satisfying, fulfilling, productive, enjoyable and totally within the will of our Heavenly Father. Therefore, we are and will continue to achieve far more than ever we would have as individuals. One and one becomes much more than two. It is amazing how God works and being in His perfect will and purpose is the most satisfying way to live. We then find more *genuine peace* in this life and ultimately an eternity of bliss in heaven. What a joy! One final point, **timing is everything**. Even when something is part of God's plan for us, it is important that we don't rush into it, try to force it or alternatively, seek to thwart or delay it in any way. This too affects our level of peace and wellbeing. I always know when this is happening for me personally, when for example the project or objective on which I am seeking to work becomes ridiculously and illogically complicated, difficult and seemingly impossible to achieve or make sense of at the time. It's when I lose my peace and ability to think clearly to solve or achieve the objective, and I begin to see clearly why this is not a good thing to do at this time. There are many examples of this in the Bible and I'm sure you can also think of situations where this has happened in your own life. **God's timing is perfect,**

Chapter 7 - Beliefs are also Enablers or Inhibitors

Have you ever thought about the degree to which our beliefs affect the level of peace, fun, joy and hope that we have in life? This chapter considers some examples in various different categories. But first, it is extremely important to note, that if we wish to enhance peace levels in our lives, what we believe should always be positive, constructive, uplifting and based on verifiable facts, or alternatively well-grounded faith. That is faith which is tried and proven from a sound interpretation and application of The Bible, together with the related personal experience and testimonies of hundreds of millions of followers of The Lord Jesus Christ across the world, including myself. There are so many examples of beliefs which have a serious impact on our lives, that it is almost impossible to do justice to the subject. I have however sought to select some which I have found to be critically important, and which hopefully will be of some assistance and benefit to you personally. This chapter lists each category or topic, describes some of the false beliefs related to that area, and the impact they might have. Then I articulate some associated truths and the benefits of ascribing to these truths, as well as other important aspects related to the topic. The first one I've chosen is the most important of all.

Jesus - Some believe that Jesus was just a man, who had a good heart and set some very fine examples of how we should live. But He is now dead and gone, and only the memory of Him lives on in the writings and recollections of other humans over the ages. This belief is clearly false. There is more evidence that Jesus lived, was crucified, died and was buried, then rose again from the dead, demonstrating that He was the Son of God, than there is of any other major historical event or person existing or living in ancient times. These events were experienced firsthand by countless eyewitnesses, including seeing Him ultimately descend into heaven. If it were not for this sacrificial and miraculous act of redemption, there would be no hope for mankind. Reconciliation could not be made between man and God, our hearts and lives could not be healed restored and set free from sin and guilt, and our wilfulness, rebellion and separation from God would be final and irreparable. Entry to heaven would not be possible since that eternal and beautiful place is sin-free. Our unredeemed spirits would not be able to enter, and certainly not be at peace there. The truth is that Jesus Christ is in fact the literal Son of God, was born into this world by miraculous virgin birth, His true Father is Jehovah God, The Almighty, and His blood line is from God Himself, and therefore pure, holy and unsullied by our polluted earthly bloodlines. So, He was therefore able to be the perfect sacrifice for our sin, pay the full price for our rebellion, conquer death and hell and rise from the dead, returning to heaven to make it possible for us to do the same. What we have to do is repent, of our waywardness and receive His gift of eternal life, now and forever. That makes us new and clean on the inside, ready for our eternal existence, but also able to achieve, with the help of His Holy Spirit, some level of holiness here in this life. This single truth when fully entered into and appropriated, brings so much peace and joy into our lives that we will never be the same again. In order to change this belief from the negative to the positive, we just need to consider the possibility that it is true and ask the Lord that if it is, to please give us faith to believe it right now, and then step out and choose to receive it, take hold of this beautiful gift, and seek to follow in His way. You will notice an immediate difference in the way you think and feel, and this will open up a whole new world for you to explore, with His help. I can personally confirm that the Judeo-Christian way is fully true in spirit and in detail; that I have personally tested the key tenets of this good news in my own life, and seen it lived out and demonstrated in the lives of thousands with whom I have journeyed on this earth. I have also explored most other major philosophies and found they all come up wanting against the Way of Christ. If you've never done so before, I challenge you to personally seek out The Way, by reaching out to Him today, studying His Book, inviting Him into your life and surrendering your future to Him. You will never be the same again and a whole new vista of enlightenment, enablement, destiny, power and purpose will open up before you. You will experience far more challenges than you have ever faced before, yet as you enter into the fullness of The Faith, and walk in obedience to the Holy Spirit, you will be able to enjoy a level of *genuine peace* which is far beyond any earthly peace, and this will enable you to enter into a new level of effectiveness, able to achieve absolutely anything that you have been asked by Him to do.

Then there is this most powerful world changing agent which Jesus modelled and encouraged His disciples to live out and spread across the whole world...

Love - Regarding beliefs about love, some would say that to show love, immediately puts one in a place of weakness and vulnerability. This belief is also generally false. If it were indeed universally true, and we all insisted upon applying our own selfish form of earthly love, then yes, we would all be taking advantage of each other, flirting, carousing, having affairs, loosely taking sex wherever we can find it, without commitment or reserve, seeking only our own personal gratification, then there would truly be no peace in this world, or in our own life. The truth is however that the love with which we are supposed to love God, ourselves and each other is described as *agape, the selfless, mindful, and committed heavenly love*, as considered at length in my third book Learning Places: Real Love. It is superior to any form of earthly love, and always operates from a place of strength and purpose. This type of love has foremost in mind the highest best good of the other party and seeks to operate consistently within thoughtful, disciplined, just and fair boundaries which do not allow abuses to occur in either direction. While always loving the other person, this form of love will consistently lead them both to identify and resist various forms of abuse, control and neglect. They will also be motivated to apply clear and wise guidelines, principles, and processes, both inside and outside of the relationship. Finally, there will always be a constant seeking and applying of strategies to help each other grow in compassion, communication, respect, wisdom and maturity. This will engender strength, depth, trust and understanding, thus serving to increase exponentially both *genuine peace* and the enjoyment of life for all parties. Which leads to...

Happiness - Positive beliefs about happiness are germane to experiencing a full and complete level of health, including spiritual, mental and physical. A general sense of wellbeing and an overall feeling of satisfaction will enhance success and enjoyment of life. This is true of the individual, the couple, family, group, community, village, city or nation. Sadly, there are two significant false beliefs about happiness, which working separately or together, are denying hundreds of millions of people the opportunity to have some semblance of joy in their life. The first is a) the belief that it is impossible to be truly happy, and secondly b) that we must continuously strive after and passionately pursue personal happiness at all costs and in all situations in order to achieve it. The former causes many of us to give up hope and disengage from life, relationships, work, hobbies and pastimes, feeling that it's all too hard and not really worth the effort. This can then cause or be accompanied by depression, melancholy, deep sadness, disappointment or discouragement. Some even become critical, cynical or suicidal, and may seek to lose themselves in substance abuse, addictions, distractions or self-gratification. These then quickly reduce and spoil one's sense of wellbeing, productivity and effectiveness, thus de-motivating the individual. If not checked and dealt with individually and in community, this malaise can easily spread across the broader community with devastating effects. There is no peace in this false belief. The latter false belief is even more prevalent and causes many to become caught up in materialism, consumerism, humanism, hedonism, and many other 'isms', which when studied closely are also seen to be counterproductive to peace and happiness for anyone including the perpetrator. Continual striving after one's own happiness usually creates a state of constant pressure, stress, striving, competition, indebtedness, and an insatiable longing for more. Worse still if allowed to take too much hold for too long in our soul, it can also develop into being miserly, greedy, self-obsessed and anti-social or alternatively proud, snobby or self-elevating. None of these characteristics will engender true peace or happiness for ourselves or those around us. I should however emphasize at this point that the pursuit of happiness is a worthy objective in life and is enshrined in the constitutions of some model nations. But it is the motivation and the ways and means which one uses to achieve happiness, and indeed what we mean by happiness, which make the specific act righteous or not. For example, I have seen couples, single mothers, fathers and orphan children living in extreme poverty in many third world countries, sometimes on or near rubbish heaps from which they glean daily in order to survive. Many live in cardboard or rough wooden enclosures with scant resources for their livelihood, yet when they have a personal relationship with Jesus, they are as happy as any people I have seen anywhere in the world. This might seem incongruous to some, but true happiness is more a state of mind, heart and spirit and not directly dependent on what we might have or not have. The truth is we can all potentially have a strong degree of happiness in our lives. It has less to do with our own personal environment and circumstances and much to do with how we think and feel and the beliefs which we allow to take hold in our soul. If we will begin to seriously believe that we can have true happiness, in the simplest of lifestyles, and passionately seek out the source and nature of such happiness, we will see much more harmony, contentment, cohesion, *genuine peace* and enjoyment in life... Largely possible due to...

The Cross - As mentioned earlier, the cross, crucifixion and resurrection of The Lord Jesus Christ holds a pivotal place in history and clearly gives humankind an opportunity for redemption and reconciliation, as well as a complete transformation of the mind, together with bounteous blessings and a whole new fresh start. The cross is the paramount and universally known representation of this eternally significant event. Three really significant false beliefs about the cross are a) it is just a good luck charm. b) It is not enough to save me, I've done far too much wrong, or c) One must accept everything which comes our way in life as a cross which we must bear. If we believe in the first, the cross will typically be used as a talisman, often hanging it in the car, on the mirrors or keyring, in the bedroom, bathroom, kitchen, caravan, or alternatively wearing it like jewellery on the ears, neck, wrist or ankle. Now there is nothing wrong in displaying a cross, it is a good testimony, remembrance, celebration and telling forth of the truth and importance of what Jesus did.

However, to believe that you will be protected by it is folly, in that the item itself has no power of its own. The true power of the cross comes from Jesus Christ and His sacrifice for us on that cross and may only be claimed and experienced if one has made a salvation covenant, and are living in some semblance of obedient, personal relationship with Him. It is also best if we are walking in His ways and principles and living according to His values, beliefs and worldview. Then the cross-event will be truly protective in our lives. Regarding the second stated incorrect belief about the cross, being insufficient to deal with our serious failings and sins. It matters not what we have done or not done in life, no matter how terrible it might have been, God the Father has decreed that the death and resurrection of His perfect Son has paid the price for the sins of all humankind, when it is entered into and taken hold of with our whole heart, soul, mind and strength, and we are seeking to love Him, be like Him and follow faithfully in His footsteps. All sinners; murderers, abusers, rapists, kidnappers, thieves, terrorists, etc. can be redeemed through submission to the salvation which is inherent in the Cross and a personal relationship with the powerful, eternal King Jesus who made it all possible. The third belief, while initially seeming to have a ring of truth about it, is also generally untrue. The concept of a 'cross' which we must bear is a risky generalization. There are occasionally some things in life which the Lord will not take away from us, at least for a time, and others that we may even have to put up with for our whole life. The truth here is that unless we get specific revelation from God himself, it is impossible for us to know what we will have to bear and that which we will eventually recover from or overcome. He is a miracle working God and can heal us and change situations supernaturally in an instant. Human beings are also creative and inventive, our body soul and spirit are marvellous creations, able to heal, recover and renew themselves with the right treatment, and there are so many natural therapies and other medications which we currently have and are still discovering that can bring about astounding recovery. So, as you can see a sound appropriation of the principles and truths of the Cross are also required and will ultimately lead us to experience truly *genuine peace*. And the power of this amazing Cross is...

Holy Spirit - Is the person, presence and power of the Godhead operating in the world today. When the Bible says Spirit of God, Spirit of Christ or Holy Spirit, these are all referring to one and the same entity, and that is the Holy Spirit. False beliefs regarding Holy Spirit are many, but some which will significantly affect our ability and potential to experience peace are a) that it is impossible to have the fullness of the Holy Spirit, to the extent that the wonderful, desirable character-enhancing fruit of the Spirit, (love, joy, peace, patience, kindness, goodness, faithfulness, gentleness and self control), will be manifest strongly and influentially in our lives, causing us to be seriously Christ-like in nature. They would say that it's all too hard, and we are not perfect. This is, however, not Biblically accurate and nor is it practically correct. I know personally that the life changing power of salvation in the Cross of The Lord Jesus Christ working together with the agency of the Holy Spirit can bring radical change for the better into our hearts. I have seen how the seemingly simple act of asking the Lord to renew my heart and give me the mind of Christ, began to radically change how I felt about circumstances, caused me to make better and wiser decisions and made me better able to love. I have learned too that a daily reading of small sections of the Bible, in a systematic way, can impart wisdom into my spirit and help me discern and internalize positive principles for living. I also quickly noticed that the learning and application of these Biblical principles was much more intuitive than academic. That while initially I was engaging with them mentally, as I read the words on the paper, spiritually and practically I was beginning to absorb something new and life changing, which began to radically affect my behaviour. I also know that any time which I spend sitting in the presence of the Spirit of God connecting, engaging, relating, seeking, searching, enquiring, repenting, praising, worshipping, sharing, dialoguing and listening, always pays massive dividends, in personal and strategic revelation, encouragement, refreshment, wisdom and ideas for action. Time spent communing, surrendering; seeking Him with all our heart and a willingness to engage and obey his perfect will, are all keys to growing strongly in the fruit of His Spirit and Godly character. It is not at all impossible to have the fullness of the fruit of Holy Spirit personally active in our lives, but rather entirely feasible and worthwhile, and with the proper motives, attitudes and actions one can appropriate all that the Lord has for us to make us more like Him every day. If fruit of the Holy Spirit were not available to us in some level of development and maturity, we could not possibly be effective agents and examples of goodness and rightness in this world. We would therefore just be adding to the negative, unloving, rebellious or self-centred behaviour which seems to be increasing in our society today, and thus adding to the general level of chaos out there in the world. It is far more beneficial for all concerned to enter into the fullness of all that God has for us, and be agents and models of His Way, giving our society every chance of obtaining *genuine peace*. Then there is the false belief that b) the gifts of the Holy Spirit are not in operation or general use today. That they were only meant for a time in the early days of the church in order to get things started. The teaching of this fallacy over the generations has been a diabolical doctrine. It has shackled the people of God, caused massive challenges and is still dealing many foul blows to church communities and individuals. You see if this belief were really true, and these amazing and potent gifts of the Holy Spirit (word of wisdom, word of knowledge, faith, healing, miracles, prophecy, discernment, tongues and interpretation of tongues) were not available for today, then we would be dangerously devoid of God's specific, contextual, heavenly wisdom, needed to solve today's plethora of overly complex challenges. We would not have specific revelation-knowledge about the devilish dilemmas we often face, but rather only our own finite and often too simplistic, biased or inaccurate thought processes. There would be no revelation or word of faith for us to confidently believe and ask for acts of God and changes in earthly circumstances which are in tune with His heart. There would be no opportunity for Divine healing only natural and medical approaches. Miracles and supernatural interventions would not be possible to action through either prayer or declaration. Prophetic ability to speak God's revelation regarding what the Bible is saying generally or about a given situation would be unavailable. The ability to speak God's words of blessing and direction into someone's life would not be possible. Ability for Him to impart to us information about the future would not be active. Discerning right from wrong, light from darkness, good from evil and the actions or intended actions of the human heart would be impossible. Finally tongues, which refers to another language which Holy Spirit can give us to speak uniquely and privately with God either consciously or unconsciously, would not be available, thus limiting our prayers to known earthly languages and denying us the ability to pray helpfully when in an earthly sense we just don't know what to pray. Furthermore, the Lord could not, as He designed it to do, use this gift to guide us in what to pray for important and urgent events, issues and people, without having to take the time to first brief us and direct us. Interpretation of tongues is the ability to understand what is being said during an utterance in the gift of tongues. Without this gift people would not be able to understand what is being said in tongues in a public meeting, thus making it of no benefit to the hearer. Without these gifts the Church would be impotent, having no power to discern and understand current situations or to act upon them supernaturally in order to make the world a better place. This would allow the chaos, which can easily be observed in the world wherever there is no constructive input of light and goodness, to increase and multiply until the pain in society became unbearable. There would ultimately be no peace, possibility of peace, or peaceful places to retreat to in order to avoid the ensuing chaos. Holy Spirit often uses heavenly agents as well...

Angels - Are God's agents for good in the heavenly realm and assist Him to fulfill His plan, purpose and destiny for all of humanity. Some false beliefs regarding angels which affect our ability to have peace are a) that they do not exist, or b) that they do exist but have very little, to no involvement in the activities of history and humankind. These are both false beliefs. Biblical records and firsthand human experience, including my own, clearly demonstrate the existence of angels. I have recorded some of these accounts in my earlier books but will add the following here and now. There are myriads of cohorts of angels that operate under heavenly command, in large and small groups. They are instantly available and fully obedient to the word of God and are agents for the fulfillment of His will. They perform the functions of warriors, guardians, messengers, watchmen and worshipers. Moving to and fro between the heavenly realm and the earthly realm as the Lord directs, they are typically invisible but can materialize at will in any form of their choice or need. As is recorded in the Bible, and many other contemporary accounts, I have received a variety of visitations and assistance from angels over the years. I have been physically and spiritually protected by their intervention in my circumstances, received important messages, been guided, encouraged, strengthened and exhorted to go on through difficult circumstances, in which they and the full agency of heaven would assist me. I have seen them appear in human form, as eagle-hawks, ghostlike smoky entities, fleeting shadows or flashes of light. Their presence is always comforting and brings a sense of peace, hope, confidence and protection. If we deny their existence or ability to help us on the journey of life our levels of peace and assurance of protection will almost certainly be adversely affected. There are also evil angels...

Demons - are renegade angels that chose to not serve God, rebelled against Him and His plan for humankind, and are actively seeking to undermine the positive work of salvation, redemption and reconciliation which God is doing in the earth. They and their leader satan, are constantly seeking to kill, steal, and destroy the good work of God and humanity. They have been judged and cast out of heaven and now roam earth and sky seeking to spoil whatever they can and take as many people as possible to hell with them in due course. They have no real power or authority, unless human beings give it to them, and one day they will receive their final judgment and sentence and ultimately be imprisoned for eternity. False beliefs regarding demons are similar to angels as follows. a) That they do not exist, b) They exist but have very little involvement in our lives and c) which is quite diabolical, that demons are not evil, but rather agents of God used to give us an evil alternative so that we have a genuine choice to test our free will choices and hone our life learning skills. If we believe a) or b) then the demons would have free reign to disturb our peace, steal, kill and destroy; or seek to deceive us into ignoring God and His ideal plan for our world. Worse still they could even try to cause us to actively rebel against God, as they themselves have done, seeking to bring us into the same judgment which they have already received. Instead of denying their existence we need to be conscious of their diabolical activities and agendas and become fully aware of all the weapons and strategies which have been provided for us to resist, overcome and be victorious against any tactics which they might use. Then there is c). demons are not evil. The big risk here is that we will underestimate their terrible plans and objectives to destroy us and will not take seriously the battle between good and evil. This will also cause us to lose our peace because the demons will still vehemently execute their devilish plans against us, but we will not have sound strategies to respond, because we are ill informed and will be easily deceived by their demonic antics. *Genuine peace* can only come from conquering these demons, no matter how big or small they might be, using the power and authority that is vested in us as sons and daughters of the living God! Weapons against demonic activity, which give us victory and peace, are for example the fruit of the Spirit which grows as a result of Christ's mind and character developing in us through the agency of His Holy Spirit. Firstly, the love of God when fully appropriated conquers fear, hatred, rebellion and other sin, thus healing broken relationships, as well as setting good boundaries in the spiritual realm, where demons may not pass. And His heavenly love in us will always desire the best outcomes for other human beings. This makes the demons sick and causes them to flee. Then joy when fully entered into will eventually overcome depression, sadness, mourning, brokenness, and will give no place to devilish mind-sets. Godly peace cannot be disturbed by demonic activity and provides a sound base from which to stand, resist and fight agents of darkness. Patience, which is an outflow of *genuine peace*, means we will not be moved into places of agitation by the presence and activities of demons. Once they see that we know and have true peace and patience, they cannot succeed in harassing us anymore. Kindness is another effective weapon against demonic activity because one of their favourite pastimes is to create circumstances to try to cause us to be unkind to one another. Whenever we feel like being unkind, beware and watch out for demonic presence and action on our heart or past memories and feelings seeking to stir up negative emotions. Forgiveness is the key to having the victory here. Goodness is another important key. If we always seek to do good, we will be instantly aware when something within us or outside of us seeks to goad us to do evil or unrighteous acts. We can then immediately repent of the wrong things which we may have done or not done in the past which have given us a weak spot in this area. Then He will give us the victory! The desire will leave, and we can begin to develop good new positive habits, and the demons will have nowhere to put the hooks into us to try to tempt us to do evil. Faithfulness is another. It is like a shield in that it protects our vital parts from demonic attack. If we are truly open, honest, transparent and act with integrity and faithfulness, being men and women of our word, demons will have nowhere to strike at us. If they try, which they inevitably do, their attacks will be fended off and exposed by our faithfulness. Gentleness is akin to kindness and works in similar ways. Self-control finally is the bringing of our body, soul and spirit; mind, will and emotions, all in line with God's spirit, heart, and character, and allowing His Godliness to govern everything we do and say and even think. Then the demons truly do have nowhere to go and will usually leave us in peace most of the time, because their efforts are wasted on us!

Then, beliefs about daily life are also key...

The Here and Now - is where we live every day of our lives, every moment, at work, at home, at school, at play, on holiday, wherever we happen to find ourselves. Some believe that a) it doesn't really matter what we do in this life. That life is short, inconsequential and generally meaningless. This point of view often comes by way of the false belief that the universe evolved by itself from nothing. Then there is b) that we should have freedom to do whatever we like without consequence. Another is c) that distracting and abstracting ourselves from the problems in life and ignoring them will give us peace, and finally d) that everything in life was fore-ordained and meant to be, we can't change anything for the better so let's just go with the flow and make the best of whatever happens. These are all false beliefs and actually under-gird many of the really serious social, mental, spiritual and psychological problems in our world today. Let's start with a) the truth is that everything we do and say in life really does matter, and will always affect ourselves, others or our environment in either a positive, peace enhancing fashion or alternatively a negative peace constraining, reducing or destroying way, and this can often be quite profound. People are always watching what we do and say and being affected by it. A child will see her parent doing something that is unhelpful or wrong and because it is her mum or dad, she will assume that is appropriate behaviour. And she will quite probably emulate or accommodate such behaviour, either now or later in life, quite possibly to her own detriment or the detriment of others. People generally decide who you are, your character, your trustworthiness, congeniality, whether they like you, or trust you, etc., by observing what you say and do, and the spirit you demonstrate at the time... This can happen in an instant and will affect ongoing relationships. So, we need to be on guard and seek to operate with loving, wise, objective, respectful, integrity. Life does have meaning and purpose, and so does each of us, and our lives are connected in a myriad of ways. I know many young people who were told by parents, teachers or authority figures in their lives, that they were dumb, and they seriously believed it was true, until eventually with the help of God and observant friends found that it wasn't true and went on to do amazing things of which they had previously assumed they were not capable. That is why b) is also not true and cannot be an option in a healthy society. We just cannot be allowed or encouraged to do whatever we want to do, whether right or wrong, because everything we do affects someone. Sadly, some people seem to want to do unhealthy, undesirable, often destructive and criminal things, and de- criminalizing their behaviour does not help. What we are typically comfortable saying and doing in our daily lives is a matter of the heart and conscience and constantly increasing legislation will not solve the problems but will only reduce the levels of peace and enjoyment in everyone's life. It is best to have a set of positive, proven accepted beliefs and values which are inculcated into our children in families, schools, workplaces and in life generally. The thesis of this book and the experience of hundreds of millions of people world-over, me included, is that the Judeo-Christian values are the ideal and proven set to achieve this outcome successfully. Any others which even though they may contain some good principles are typically drawn from the Judeo- Christian foundation, so why not go directly to the source which contains the entire philosophy of life as well as the power to redeem, restore and not just brush over the problems. Regarding c), this belief is an attempt to achieve peace by abstracting ourselves away from the problem, ignoring it, or focusing on something else in order to distract ourselves away from the issue. This might sound viable, but it isn't, it is only sweeping the issue 'under the carpet' and over time this approach usually makes the matter worse, more destructive to peace and more difficult to resolve. If something is endangering or destroying our level of peace it is worthy of remedial attention. And whether we are reading the situation correctly or not, the fact that our peace is being affected is an important issue. Setting our mind and heart to analysing the situation, finding mutually agreeable solutions, working through related issues honestly and vulnerably is always worth the effort. Such endeavours will always lead to *genuine peace* as long as both parties are being objective, and considering all of the relevant issues, with an attitude of believing that they themselves may be wrong in some areas, and having a willingness to make changes where appropriate. Finally, d) that everything is fore-ordained is a belief that if it were true, would make putting effort into life, seeking to make the world a better place, totally futile. It postulates that life just happens to us as it were, we have no control over it and no ability to influence it. What a negative, destructive, soul-destroying philosophy and belief. No wonder we have drug issues, hopelessness, selfishness, fatalism, suicide and such, running rife in our society. The truth is that God is absolutely Sovereign and able to do or not whatever he chooses. He knows exactly what is going on in His world at anytime and anywhere. He can see the future as easily as the past and is always able to tell exactly what will happen. Nevertheless, He chooses to give us free will within reasonable bounds, and allows, in fact He encourages our good efforts to change things, and hopefully make the world a better place. This making-things-better is a very satisfying endeavour. It is what we were actually designed for and is even more effective and fulfilling if we are conducting ourselves generally within the overall values, principles, belief systems and specific goals, objectives and plans which God has for our world. This truly brings *genuine peace* because our efforts are enabled by the power of His Holy Spirit, provided for by the God of Heaven, and in tune with His will and plan, being led and championed by King Jesus. His will and plan is to progressively bring the Kingdom of God into being here on earth, and prepare as many people as possible to become Godlike in nature, to be able to rule and reign here and now and when he returns, as well as be ready for heaven, the ultimate reward, when the time comes. What a joy!

And then there is the afterlife...
Eternity - is what we will step into when we die or are translated by God to be ready for our heavenly existence. When this happens, our earthly bodies will become fully spiritual in nature and substance and ready and able to move in that spiritual dimension. Beliefs about eternity are many. Let's consider some:-
a) That there is no eternity. We just live this life and then it's all over. Our existence ceases and we have no more self-awareness, in this life or anywhere else, and are simply snuffed out like a candle. Then b) that there

is an eternity but it's just more of the same, with both good and evil, on the other side, in another realm, and maybe that there is a possibility we will one day return to this earthly type of existence. And finally, c) That there is an eternity, but it may or may not be a very nice place to which we are going or being sent. Well yes you guessed it! None of these are true, and if they were there would be no possibility of *genuine peace* in this life. For example, a) would easily lead to thinking why should we bother? There is no meaning or purpose, no enduring aspect to this existence, nothing worth learning, worth working for or fighting for. Why bother resisting temptation or developing self control, raising a family, exploring destiny, building dynasty or creating value, worth or inheritance? An understandably miserable existence would follow this belief. b) is similarly disconcerting in that while there is deemed to be an eternity, there is no hope of salvation, redemption, character improvement, growth toward perfection, the containment, eradication and destruction of evil, etc. Just more of the same battle with good and evil, over and over again, and for eternity. Well, there's no peace there either! And finally, c) an uncertain eternity is a shocking prospect, filled with unknowns and uncertainties, living life with no foundations, no guideposts, values and no hope of reward, or positive outcomes... And after it's all over there is only the strong possibility of meeting a terrible end. I have seen people labouring in life under this false belief and it is a terrible existence. Indeed, why would one want to live anyway? I also have friends who often have the privilege of sitting with people when they are dying. They relate consistently that people who have a personal relationship and faith in the Lord Jesus Christ, typically approach death with peace and dignity, looking forward to meeting their saviour and the saints that have gone before. They slip away quietly when their time comes, and this overwhelming sense of *genuine peace* at their point of death is such a beautiful thing to experience, and to share with someone. It is also a powerful testimony to the power and reality of the gospel. Alternatively, those who haven't met Jesus and given their life to Him and His cause are usually overcome with anxiety, fear or dread as they prepare to meet their end. Nevertheless, God is still most gracious and there is a solution should someone find themselves in this place. Even on our death bed in the last few moments of our lives, it is possible to repent and find peace with God and receive the redemptive gift of salvation of the Lord Jesus Christ. Such is His patience, long suffering, grace and love for us that He will receive us and make peace with us, and we can be born again and filled with His Holy Spirit even at the point of death, just before we pass into eternity.

Beliefs about 'self as a human race also matter...
Man - the male form of humankind who have collectively been given the mandate together with the women, to responsibly steward the whole earth in an effective and Godly manner. This includes objectives such as establishing and maintaining freedom, justice, mercy, orderliness, safety, security, fairness, respect, sharing of resources, valuing human life, ensuring durability of existence, an atmosphere of peaceful living and potential for constant improvement, etc. Many things have worked against this worthy and mandatory objective. Worthy because it is self-

evidently laudable and obvious that it needs to be achieved, or else anarchy and chaos would rule the earth. The objectives are also mandatory because if we were to fail, our global society would likely destroy itself in one way or another. Sadly, from the beginning humanity rebelled against God and His magnificent master plan, which was always necessary for our betterment. Things got so bad He sent a global flood to destroy all but just a handful of righteous men and women in order to give us another chance. We stumbled again after this event, in that once we came out of the ark, which had saved us from the flood we just stayed in one area and multiplied and grew in skills, education and economy but not in character or faith. Hearts were still black as coal and bent on selfishness and evil. God then came down and dispersed the one language into many, to force the people to progressively scatter across the whole earth according to these new language groups. It is said the sons of Noah initially migrated as follows, Ham went to Africa, Japheth to Europe and Shem to Asia. But we still had not attended to our characters. Then He set a redemption plan in place, which He had in mind from the beginning because he knew we would struggle. The plan was to choose a righteous man Abraham and build his tribe into a nation, Israel and from this nation bring the saviour, Jesus Christ, the son of God and the son of David, into the world to give us one perfect chance at redemption. This event then spawned Judeo-Christianity which began to spread across the whole earth. This happened and is still happening today, by the agency of faithful men and women, operating in the power of the Holy Spirit and under the mandate of the Lord Jesus Christ. The Bible says that once every tribe and tongue and nation has had opportunity to hear His message of redemption, and a chance to respond or reject King Jesus, then He will return to the Earth in visible and bodily form to implement His final solution, *genuine peace* for all who will receive this Good News!

Now returning for a closer study of some peace related beliefs regarding man, and by implication woman, for example a) that we are not up to the task, that we will fail, and the world will go to hell in a sinking ship. b) We can solve the problems we face as a society all by ourselves, and that we don't need God's help thank you very much! Or c) that a man individually has to be strong and independent, with limited emotion, no tears, a clear thinking, tough nut, able to solve all his own problems and those for whom he is responsible, by himself without the need to confide in, or get assistance from others and the like. And finally, d) that men are often angry, bossy, authoritarian, and independent, opinionated, hard hearted, unloving, uncaring and so forth. Well, while seemingly plausible in some aspects, these generalizations are also largely untrue... And when men... together with women are truly born again and seek to walk in obedience with God and surrender their carnal nature to Him, the exact opposite becomes possible and amazing world changing results can be achieved.

There is a heavenly plan which is well defined and well known among God-fearing followers of our Lord, Jesus Christ, regarding methods and approaches which will give us success, as individuals, couples, families, communities, cities and nations. These are all the principles, processes, guidelines and methods which typically under-gird the good and righteous aspects of western civilization, and other nations which have successfully applied these principles in their societies. Furthermore, we don't have to be islands unto ourselves, working alone, isolating ourselves away. Nor do we have to be doomed to negative and harsh opinions and authoritative behaviour. The miraculous inner healing aspects of the gospel of our Lord Jesus, together with the presence of strong, wise and loving fathers and male role models in their life, along with mature advisers, mentors, good and Godly mates, and finally the availability of specialist training where necessary, men will usually rise to their highest potential. They are designed to be good hearted independent and yet inter-dependent, strong but gentle leaders working together with likeminded people to achieve good outcomes. And we can also be assured that there is a gospel pattern full of good news and viable, tried and true methods which can be implemented along with the person and power of God's Holy Spirit, which will help guide us all to achieve a degree of separate yet heavenly synchronized like-mindedness, sufficiently able to bring a strong level of *genuine peace* into this world. Yes, there is still a magnificent hope and profound chance of success for our world, particularly as our men harness the God-given power of our complementary male and female genders to work together for good.

Woman - the female version of humankind. Women are also designed to work individually or as teams in concert with others, and this is also meant to achieve

Godly outcomes for our world. They can work both independently and strategically, when they have the appropriate gifting and calling, and are capable of providing the most amazing complement to men, particularly their marriage partners, as well as in teams with projects, businesses, schools etc. This miraculous ability which a woman has to support her man in a covenant marriage is truly marvellous, and both God designed and ordained. She can make her man so profoundly more productive and effective, when well matched in a mutually gifted complementary marriage partnership. Women are also equally capable, along with other men to lead, operate and support each other in productive and effective teams, whether they are married or single. Some false beliefs regarding women are the same as a) and b) for man above, that they are not up to the task of making the world a better place or that they can do it themselves without God's help, and the countermanding truths are similar to that of the men. Another is c) that women are the weaker of the sexes. Nothing could be further from the truth. Although they can, and are designed to be tender, emotional and nurturing, which is necessary for some of their myriad roles in life, they can also be the strongest, smartest, hardest working, most courageous, enduring, determined, valiant beings on earth. Furthermore, their natural gifts of mothering, soothing, nurturing, gathering and effective, affirming and connecting communication, are imperative in working towards *genuine peace* in a family, community or society. Finally, some suggest d) that behaviour at times ascribed to women can sometimes be moody, uptight, angry, nagging, manipulative, bitchy, divisive, gossips or the like. Well as for the negative behaviours mentioned for men above, ladies who grapple with any of these types of issue, can be free of them and certainly do not have to remain captive to them. With a personal relationship with our Lord Jesus Christ, the inner healing beauty and power of this redemptive alliance, along with wise Godly role models, both women and men, can effectively and soundly overcome any and all of these types of behaviours. My lovely wife Kathy often reminds me that if we will just read the word of God, listen to the voice of God and be willing to do what He says, we can overcome any short coming in our lives. He knows us best, knows what and how we need to change, can explain it to us in words that we understand, and also give us the heavenly assistance and power we need in order to make the change. He can help us to remove anything from our lives which is causing trouble, aggravating, or captivating us within, and ultimately set us free. This usually involves repentance, and saying that we are sorry, rejecting the spirit which may be behind the behaviour, and asking the Lord Jesus to set us free, and protect us from returning to it, or allowing it to return. It's interesting to observe that many of the negative characteristics mentioned in these sections for both men and women are often counterfeits, opposites or aberrations of the positive characteristics which we are each meant to demonstrate. This clearly shows another of the wiles which demons seek to use, in turning us against ourselves and actually trying to turn our strengths into weaknesses. It should be noted too that because women tend to be more verbal in their relationships, something else which can cause or aggravate these types of feeling or behaviour, is when a woman does not have someone to share with and confide in, to process all that she may be feeling at the time. She may therefore not feel listened to, really heard, or understood, supported, loved, valued or appreciated. In an ideal marriage this is a key role for the husband to aspire to and seek to fulfill by demonstrating honour, love and appreciation through connecting at this heart level. Both men and women may even have other basic needs which have not been met in their lives, ideas, dreams, opinions, worries, fears or feelings which have not been given a second thought or even allowed to be shared. Exploring and working through these types of issues significantly enhances the possibility of achieving *genuine peace*. I think you get the idea. This journey, this way of communicating and interacting with each other will help revolutionize our marriages and relationships and increase our mutual enjoyment of life and each other. Another more serious possibility, which is really important, and can sometimes be the case, is that some of these behaviours for both male and female may have come about inside the heart, because they feel like they have, or actually have been... abused, abandoned, neglected, betrayed or rejected sometime in life, or because their partner has been unfaithful. These are very serious issues... but with appropriate personal or vicarious, listening, openness, transparency, honesty, empathy, prayer, repentance, apology, forgiveness, and ultimately a making good, and a fresh start, all of these situations can be overcome. This process, along with the help and guidance of the Lord Jesus, usually also requires the support and wise confidential assistance of a trusted, true and Godly friend/s, counsellor or pastor. More on this topic is contained in Chapter 8, and as said before once genuine comprehensive inner healing has taken place, and oneness achieved in our hearts, and with those around us, our potential is unlimited and *genuine peace* will flow into and through our lives and the world at large.

Then there is the next generation...

Children - are such an important part of life, marriage, family, community, city and nation. They have the potential to bring us so much exuberant joy, and yet sometimes the deepest of heartache, and all the flavours of emotion in between. They truly enrich our lives, teach us so many things, and help us learn to deal with all the different shades and nuances of life experience. Regarding children some people believe a) that it's not worth having children, the complexity, sorrow, pain and cost is too high, or b) it's good to have children but it doesn't matter who raises them. Let someone else look after them, be their nanny, mind them in creche, educate them and so forth, so we don't have to worry about them, just enjoy the fact that we have children. And some say c) why would anyone want to bring children into this crazy, dark, sick, screwed up world. Or d) children are born perfect and they only get corrupted by our 'uninformed' parenting styles and behaviour, the assumption being that we should let the 'professionals' (the state, community or village) raise them because we are or maybe incompetent or incapable. And finally, e) that strong fair discipline and firm boundaries are bad for children, and we should give them lots of freedom and scope to self-determinate. Once again these are all false beliefs and are tragically affecting our functionality and effectiveness as communities and nations, as well as the levels of peace and joy in our families and societies.

Let's explore these false beliefs as a group rather than individually. Firstly, children are an amazing blessing from God Himself and meant for the building of loving and Godly families, the development of strong wise and mature men and women of God, the enjoyment of life, preparation for eternity in heaven and development of strong viable God-fearing communities and nations here on earth. Oh yes, raising children is a challenging and onerous responsibility, yet it also has the potential to be one of the most rewarding, fulfilling experiences one can have in this earthly existence. Ask any parent when they see their newborn baby for the first time, experience the developments and achievements of their young children, or watch them grow into young men and women full of dreams, goals and passion for life. Then there are the weddings and the arrival of grandchildren. And those days which often follow years of consternation and challenge, when our innocent, sometimes confused and dependent children, necessarily become adults, peers, equals and ultimately and ideally, friends on the journey. These are such delightful times to be celebrated and enjoyed to the full. Even though there is inevitably pain and sorrow, these difficult events are meant to hone and grow our life skills and experience, build stronger familial bonds, and teach us foundationally important things like compassion, grace, forgiveness and wisdom. Furthermore, it does matter, and matter critically, who raises our children. The very best people to parent our children are both their male and female natural blood parents. No one else will have the degree of passion, purpose and sense of destiny, dynasty and selflessness, to raise them in the way they are meant to. Most natural parents will do an exemplary job, and yes even though not perfect, can all learn and develop the necessary skills as they go. Parents will typically have the best intentions for their children, and not want to treat them like experimental playthings for the enjoyment or manipulation of others, or to allow them to grow up as spoiled brats with a sense of entitlement. They won't want to use them as 'cannon fodder' for social manipulators or radical minority lifestyle lobbyists. Their intentions will be positive, constructive and conservative, using tried and true parenting and education styles which have stood the test of time. They will not sacrifice their children to the 'gods' of philosophical hypotheses, pop psychological theories, political agendas like Marxist-Leninist socialism, the deconstruction of marriage and family values, or the dilution of morals and integrity. And if society can get back to positive and proactive parenting, with sound proven values, strong, wise, consistent boundaries and fair and just discipline, with minimal state interventions, then most children will respond and develop capably into mature, wise, sensible, men and women. They will feel loved, appreciated and bonded into family, as well as being more confident friends to others and valued community members, having an increasingly mature level of common sense, and a more robust understanding of what is right and wrong, just and reasonable. This will steadily increase the levels of *genuine peace* in our society, and the world will be much less crazy than it is today. It will help counteract the social, political, psychological and lifestyle experiments which are beginning to increase chaos, independence, rebellion, selfishness and an anything goes attitude and way of life. The way we raise our children is critical to the current and future viability, peace and effectiveness of our society. This is a massive topic but suffice to say that significant elements of the methodologies being taught for raising children in this generation are not working, or worse still are actually counterproductive and regressive, making family life, culture and *genuine peace* more difficult. We would do well to apply more of the simple more traditional and well-disciplined methodologies and less of the laissez faire, anything goes, free reign type approaches.

Then there is the heart of the family...

Husband and Wife - Effective fulfilling marriages and families are also paramount to the future of our nations, and it is difficult to raise children well when our marriage relationships are not strong and enduring. Healthy marriages increase the possibility of healthy families and give our society the best chance of success. The concept and covenant of marriage is coming under violent and ill-informed attack right now as we speak. Some false beliefs about this pivotal foundational relationship are that a) marriage is not worth the effort, it costs too much, and the level of self-surrender, sacrifice and complexity are just too great. That b) it is impossible to achieve true harmony and mutually intimate, honouring, mature, gracious, thoughtful, kind, respectful, loving connection in marriage, because men and women are just too different one from the other, and the pressures and responsibilities of marriage and family are too great. Or c) we can water down, redefine and corrupt the concept of marriage without losing its critical benefit to society. And d) more than fifty percent of marriages will fail anyway so why bother. That e) promiscuity and infidelity are acceptable and have minimal effect on marriage. And f) one or the other or both spouses must lose themselves in the relationship in order to make it work. And finally, g) true happiness can never be found in marriage, and so on. Well, I have excellent news to report. A good, sound, enjoyable and mutually beneficial marriage, entered into for life, is a very real and eminently achievable dream and goal. When both partners work personally, together with each other, and with the Lord God, on growing and maturing as individual people, and helping each other grow in their own couple-relationship, and with the world around them, marriage can be such a fulfilling and satisfying delight. Yes, there is always some tension and stress on the way, but the effort is truly worthwhile. Persisting and honouring each other in quality open honest vulnerable two-way conversation, until we both feel heard and fully understood is the foundation. No one party should ever be slave or subservient to the other. The workloads and responsibilities should be shared in an optimal fashion that works best for the couple, depending on their individual skills, gifts and talents. And no individual is the 'boss', in that the leadership is shared with each other in mutual respect and deference. Yes, men and women are radically different one from the other, but this is by design and not by some random accident of evolution. We were designed for different roles in life and to be able to complement, support, love and team together, but not to compete, be jealous, covetous, controlling or manipulative of each other, or have constant unconstructive conflict one with the other. To be sure, marriage and family life can be complex and challenging, but this is not meant to break us but rather make us. When we take one day at a time, invite the presence and wisdom of God, and don't worry and become stressed, but in everything make our requests and issues known to the Lord, then the *genuine peace* of God, which passes understanding, will guard our hearts and our minds, and He will make a way. Furthermore, we cannot, indeed must not, toy around with the concept of marriage, as if it were ours to do so. It is crafted perfectly and designed by our Maker to be the very fabric of our society. It is perfect in form, concept and process, and cannot be other than between a man and a woman in covenant relationship one with the other. They are meant to be the natural parents and grandparents etc., of new offspring, and to give each further generation positive identity, values, beliefs and worldview, as well as a sense of belonging, family, community, example, model, mentoring, life skills and so many other things. These can be achieved in other ways, but they can never be as effective, fulfilling and life enhancing as being actively involved in a healthy, natural family with both father and mother. And the fact that some marriages fail does not mean the concept is flawed, or that it should be cast aside as irrelevant. There can be many extenuating circumstances which lead to breakdown, but the ideal remains, and this model is still the very best family foundation for humankind. And by the way, more than half our marriages do not fail. In fact, well over seventy percent succeed with the children being raised in their own natural families. Furthermore, in certain positive environments like Judeo-Christian communities, survival rates can actually be much higher, for example in the eighty and ninety percentage point range. It's important to note however, that some families will inevitably breakdown and this should not be a place of denigration or recrimination, but rather a time to seek God and humanity for the hope of redemption, with a view to making the best of a difficult situation and recovering as much as possible from the brokenness, while seeking maximum healing and restoration for all. Finally, promiscuity and infidelity do damage marriage, often irrevocably. They are a betrayal of trust, a taking of advantage, and an abuse, perpetrated against the ones we are supposed to love. The price is too high and there are typically no enduring positive outcomes. It's just not worth it. On the other hand, fidelity, intimacy, honour, love and trust bring a great reward of true happiness, peace and joy, and lay strong foundations for *genuine peace*. It should also be noted though, that true repentance, a change of heart and behaviour, along with emotional recovery and forgiveness as well as the Divine healing of God's Holy Spirit, and a positive attitude by all parties, can ultimately bring about a full restoration and redeem the effects of indiscretion or infidelity.

Now, for the sake of completeness we must mention...
Family - which is the fruit and outcome of the abovementioned commitments and covenant relationships with each other and is well described both here and in all my other books.

Then, there is life in general...
Life - Our daily life grows out of who we are and what we do. It is the sequential and aggregate outworking of all the events, words, actions, learning, motivations, and attitudes of the years of our earthly existence.

Some false beliefs in this area which affect our peace are a) Life is not worth living. b) Life was meant to be easy. c) There is too much evil and heartache in the world to be able to enjoy life. Let me say first of all, regarding this topic, that I am hopeful that having read this book, if you have previously believed any of the above untruths, you will have discovered sufficient hope and information in order to reconsider. The gift of life is so wonderful that it is worth fighting for! We are aware of our own existence, we can think, feel, see, hear, smell, touch, taste, sense, believe, connect with the eternal, dream, create, work, play, have babies, laugh, cry, enjoy, multiply, occupy and explore the world at large. What a delight! And by now I'm also sure you can see that most of the evil in this world is something we can address, and modify, and cause this world to be a much better place, full of *genuine peace* and exuberant Joy!

Let's explore some of these aspects...

Self and Senses - Our 'self' is the essence, core, spirit, heart of who we are. It is the God-like part of our being. The part that is self-aware, can think, dream, create and envision. I have spoken much on this in my earlier books and will just add a few more paragraphs on the topic at this point. The primary false belief about our self is that a) we are all inherently good and not needing of redemption or coaching in this regard, that most of us will naturally do the right thing and can be trusted and relied on to do such. Well sadly there is nothing further from the truth, and to believe that of ourselves and of others is one of the major sources of trouble in our world. The fact is that prior to receiving God's redemption in Christ Jesus into our spirit this part of us is 'broken' or atrophied as it were. Limited, constrained, flawed and prone to error, rather than right thinking and action. This is because we have not yet been renewed (born again), so that we can become God-like in nature and activate our ability to connect and relate to Him personally. To think otherwise always puts one into a losing situation in that we assume we'll always do what is right, and then find that we can't. Alternatively, if we trust that everyone else will do right by us, and by others, we will also be disappointed, again and again, and be taken advantage of endlessly. It has become obvious to me over the years that in order to obtain *genuine peace* we must be born again. Furthermore, we need to have experienced a large and pervasive degree of inner healing, so that our 'brokenness' and inner hurts do not distort the way we see others, or process events and circumstances, and respond and relate to the world around us. Our senses too need to be redeemed and governed righteously by our redeemed spirit. This includes such things as not allowing what we see, hear, smell, taste, touch or discern in the spirit to inappropriately tempt, influence or control us. Being born again, filled with His Spirit and like Him in nature, thought and behaviour, is a critical key to achieving *genuine peace*. And this gives us a fighting chance of always seeking to, wanting to, and being able to do that which is right in the eyes of God and man.

It is so important how we see and relate to others...
Others - are all the people in the world apart from one's self. And it is imperative that we learn to observe, discern and reflect accurately with the help of Holy Spirit, and engage, interact and relate

appropriately, with all whom we meet on the journey of life. Effective interaction with others requires the establishment of appropriate boundaries in the relationship with the other person. These need to reflect both our own core values, beliefs and worldview, together with our observations and discernment of the maturity, trustworthiness and capabilities of the other person. One must on the one hand protect our own vital self, from wounding, abuse or disadvantage, while also seeking to be appropriately open, honest, transparent and forthright enough to ensure effective communication. This is often a difficult challenge in the beginning, depending on the issues involved with both parties, but is worth the effort, and usually, eventually, with the help of God our Father, will bring a positive outcome and *genuine peace*. It goes without saying that in order to achieve a strong degree of peace in the world around us, a majority of the 'others' in our world will also need to achieve a state of *genuine peace*. This is why once we are able to achieve any reasonable level of relationship with the 'others' in our world, we need to magnanimously and lovingly share with them the secrets of this book, which are largely Biblical principles, and an accurate representation of the Judeo-Christian way of life. This is so that they might also enjoy the same blessings that we do. To do otherwise would do them an injustice, and cause us to be held accountable, by them or by others, that we did not show them The Way to *genuine peace*.

Now, a combination of 'self and 'others' leads us to community...

Us / Community - All human beings desire, in fact

yearn, consciously or subconsciously for this concept of 'community'. Seeking to belong and be a part of something bigger than ourselves... contributing, cooperating, and experiencing fellowship and fulfillment, and making the world a better place. In community all the above principles need to apply, and incidence of false beliefs must be identified, clarified, resolved and removed. A key false belief regarding community is that a) It is easy to get along in a community. Anyone can do it. One just needs the right set of rules and laws. Sadly, this is not true. Even blood family members and like-minded homogenous communities of people find it difficult to achieve a high level of harmony and peace in their group. Let alone heterogeneous collections of people such as multicultural, multi-religion, multi- philosophy or multi-sectarian groups. This difficulty in achieving a degree of consensus or unity in goals and purposes can occur for many reasons. One is that we are basically selfish beings and usually put our own needs and wants ahead of others. Our different cultures, values and background experiences bring us all to a different place in the way we think, act and conduct ourselves. What we believe is appropriate and what is not can create conflict. A classic and very real example is a culture/s which believes that anyone who is different from 'us' can be lied to, deceived in order to achieve an outcome, and in due course murdered at will, without legal repercussion, unless they recant and join the 'us'. Worse still, having joined or always been a part of the 'us', one is ostracized, persecuted or murdered if they desire to leave, or actually do leave. There are variations on this theme, but this is a very real example, and highlights why such belief systems are inappropriate, and the impossibility of integration and harmony with other groups without these same types of dubious values. Even an homogenous grouping of people often does not achieve this goal of group cohesion. As mentioned earlier, sound, robust, durable unity comes down to having a consistent set of values, beliefs and a worldview which is actually viable, proven and applied across the whole group. It also has to create an environment of mutual respect, honour and agape love for one another, as well as passionate submission to the One True and Living God, His Gospel and His Way. Any lesser strategy will always be fraught with conflicts, differing opinions and tensions of values, beliefs and worldview. I am hopeful that once this book has been read in its entirety, that this concept will become clear.

Next are some key groups of 'others' in society...
Race - Refers to the unique and particular people groups present here on earth. Sometimes a nation may consist of predominantly one people group, but this is less common in these modern times of international travel, business, economics, commerce, trade, education, migration and the occasional arbitrary assignment of national boundaries over the millennia. Many of the issues mentioned previously also apply to the practicalities of achieving peace within intra-race, multi-race and inter-race situations. A current false belief about race and racial harmony is that everyone can keep doing all that we currently typically do, according to our own traditional norms, values and beliefs, and that as long as we are kind and respectful and allow each other to continue to do so, that all will be sweet and wonderful. The truth is however, that

experience is proving this is not so, mainly because of all the conflicting and opposing beliefs that there are in our respective racial cultures. There are in fact very few viable options for bringing *genuine peace* into a multi-racial situation. In fact, in any multi- cultural situation, trying to legislate harmony by way of rules, regulations, laws, conventions, punishments, repercussions and red tape, in isolation from any other positive changes in spirit, heart, values, beliefs, and worldview, will not achieve desired genuinely peaceful outcomes. No matter how strongly they may be enforced. Human beings are designed to desire freedom, and we will yearn, dream and inevitably and inexorably work towards wanting, feeling and being truly free. We will eventually push back against anything which seeks to unduly or unjustly control, restrict or manipulate, particularly if we can see that the laws are biased, unjust or non-viable. This is why totalitarian nations and empires inevitably fall under the weight of their own injustice and inequity. Genuine racial peace requires that both physical and spiritual realities of difference need to be addressed comprehensively and cohesively in our societies. It is not possible to omit certain elements and requirements, or to add conflicting overlays in order to be politically correct or show superficial sensitivity, because that will flaw the whole process and ultimately lead to chaos. It becomes unworkable. Please bear with me, this topic of *genuine peace* is an enormously broad and complex matter to unfold and expound, and I pray your diligence in reading it to the end will be worth the investment.

Now follows the mutually agreed concept which covers everything there is...

The Universe - Is the cosmos in which our planet and planetary system operates. While we still know very little about our universe, our knowledge is increasing apace with time and technology improvement. One false belief about our cosmos is that it came about by random chance and did not and does not require an architect and overseer in order to operate effectively. The truth is that our universe is not itself God, as some would promulgate, but rather His masterful creation, operating at His design and behest. Infinitely, amazingly beautiful and unfathomable, our universe is a multi-faceted entity operating in an orderly and disciplined fashion. Its governing laws are not yet fully known or understood. All we can do is study it, marvel at its wonders, try to understand it, and seek to work with its laws in order to harness and leverage its assets and capabilities in effective ways... for the betterment of mankind. The cosmos does not need human involvement in order to exist or operate... and if we don't disturb its order and beauty unduly, it will serve as a great adventure and a set of endless knowledge horizons for us to explore during our lifetimes and future generations.

One of the most beautiful planets in this vast cosmos is 'our' Earth which is inhabited by many nations embodying a vast variety of races and languages...

Nations - are very similar in concept and in practice to races above and most countries actually have multiple races as part of their local demography. There are many false beliefs which negatively affect the peace within a nation and between nations, but I will refer here to just a few. For example, some believe that a) nations must surrender their sovereignty to an international government in order to take an effective role in the global community. b) A patriotic, nationalistic, 'home-team', pride-in- country type attitude to our own home country is counterproductive to local and global harmony. c) Because most nations contain multiple religions, that a workable national and international philosophy must include either an 'any religion is ok', a secular 'no religion' approach or a 'hybrid man-made religion' for everyone to use. d) A liberal democratic political system will work with this 'anything goes' type of culture. e) One can use legislation to enforce orderly and peaceful behavioural compliance within a nation. f) It is feasible to teach, encourage or allow citizens to believe that we can have whatever we want in life, do whatever we want to do, that we can seek our own way in everything, to the exclusion of all others, and still achieve an harmonious national existence. g) People will be happy and harmonious to be just the same as everyone else, with no potential to improve, get ahead, or better oneself in life circumstances. h) Citizens will be happy and peaceful living under controlling, draconian, authoritarian leaders and governments as long as they get their basic needs provided and are suitably occupied and entertained.

Well, I'm sure you are not surprised to note that none of these, often deeply entrenched beliefs are in fact true. The real truth regarding nations is that a) an international government would be too large and remote from real life to be relevant and helpful in seeking to create a peaceful world. There is also an inordinate risk in putting great power in the hands of so few. It is a much better and safer model to distribute controls to the national level. The best we can do is to develop agreed international standards and approaches which are practical and workable and provide incentives to nations to implement them locally. This would be a minimum set of standards with maximum flexibility and dispensation to act locally while ensuring nations work together on aspects which are important. Core areas of banking, finance, legal, political, educational, family, welfare and business processes would be examples where consistency would be required. b) It is thoroughly sound to encourage each nation to preserve an individual identity, market its own unique image, manage its sovereignty, work to its strengths, create its own set of specialties, products and services, be self-sufficient in all the basic needs of its society, but willing to trade and develop mutually beneficial coalitions with other nations. Always seeking to build cohesiveness, camaraderie, honesty and generosity toward others, as well as encouraging a strong sense of self and national esteem, and a healthy environment of competition between nations. c) Regarding religions, as concluded earlier, all religions are not equal. Many are actually counter-productive to a peaceful society. Some teach violence, dominance, control and submission with no room for creativity, spontaneity, freedom, fun, hope and joy. Others encourage an abstract distant approach to life and problems, postulating that if we ignore everything and divert our attention away from the issues, it will reduce our stress and make things more palatable. But this just allows things to deteriorate because nothing is ever addressed or resolved. Some just try to placate the 'gods' in the hope that they will stop harassing the adherents. This too is futile because the 'gods' are not God, but usually demons or other dubious spirits with other non-peaceful agendas in mind. Regarding the 'no god at all' situation, there is usually an agenda for an elite group of people to control and manipulate the populace, thus there is no room for a philosophy that teaches other agendas. The State is deemed to be 'god'. Alternatively, others who espouse that there is no God, usually know in their heart of hearts that there is a God but either don't want to admit it and thus have to consider surrendering to His sovereignty, or they are angry with God and think that if they say that He doesn't exist, that will put Him in his place and demonstrate their contempt of him. Finally, all attempts to create a common hybrid religion have failed as well due to the inconsistencies, incompatibilities and inadequacies of individual elements. **None of these types of religions can therefore be the foundation of a society which is seeking *genuine peace*. The one and only workable candidate is the pure form of Judeo-Christianity. It has all the attributes necessary to achieve true peace, when it is taught, lived and applied properly in our societies.** Sadly, there are even some pockets of false religions portraying to be a form of Judeo-Christianity, which are clearly misleading and ineffective because they have strayed from the true heart of the faith. Some have perpetrated atrocities in Jesus name, others say He is not the son of God or did not rise from the dead, did not die for the sins of mankind and do not teach the truths of the bible etc. *Genuine peace* is only possible within the pure Bible-based form of Judeo-Christianity. d) Liberal democratic 'anything goes' approach doesn't work either. If we all truly have the freedom to do whatever we like without e.g., Judeo-Christian principles underlying our personal values, conscience and societal norms, then anarchy and selfishness would quickly take hold and destroy any possibility of harmony. The 'law of the jungle' would typically begin to apply in that the strongest and most aggressive and powerful would usually win. e) History and experience have also clearly shown that one cannot bring about good behaviour through legislation alone. It requires the under-girding support and guidance of a set of positive values and a complementary belief system, which has been inculcated personally and throughout society. f) As noted above, putting our own personal goals and agendas before those of everyone else is a sure way to destroy a society. We would all just become takers and not givers, feasting off the generosity and benevolence of others, using and taking advantage, but not giving anything in return back into our society. To help bring *genuine peace* for our nation we need to have a fair, just and honourable balance between aiming for and achieving our own goals by way of self-improvement, healthy ambition and the like, yet without taking unfair advantage of others. g) In societies where everyone is supposedly 'equal', like communism, there is no incentive to work, volunteer or better one's self, unless you become an agent of the ruling elite. Yet even within the 'elite' there is no opportunity for peace because of the demonic structure and belief system which underlies the model. There is no opportunity for creativity or entrepreneurial spirit. Jealousy in a sense becomes a state 'virtue' in that citizens are encouraged to spy on each other to ensure no one is allowed to get advantage above another. This creates a deep and sinister tension amongst the people, a lack of hope and purpose and spoils any vestige of peace which seeks to emerge. h) And finally, many of the above approaches to operating a nation either require or degenerate into draconian and authoritarian styles of government, which will not, indeed cannot, foster, support or bring about a truly *genuine peace*.

Also, on the topic of peace regarding nations, there is one specific country deserving special mention due to its unique characteristics...

Israel -You might think it an unusual subject to be placed on a list of topics which can be said to enhance or inhibit peace. The reason it is included here is because Israel is God's chosen or model nation, through which he saw fit to demonstrate the key elements of both positive and negative nationhood, and the journeys and issues involved in moving toward the ideal. Israel did many things which God was not happy about and disciplined them soundly as a result. But he also blessed them when they were righteous and generally favoured them as His chosen ones. We can learn powerful truths from studying God's dealings with this amazing nation.

Some false beliefs regarding Israel, which affect our general state of peace, are a) they are outcasts which God has rejected. b) He has lost hope in them and is finished dealing with them. c) They are small and of no consequence in the scheme of things. d) Other nations are free to judge and discriminate against them and treat them harshly without consequence.

The truth about Israel however is that a) they have finished with their times of being exiles and outcasts as a result of individual and national sin, and are now coming into their season of redemption, restoration and glory. The lessons Israel learned on this journey hold the keys to the redemption, salvation and peace of our own nations and are all clearly articulated in the Bible. This is not to say that the nation is perfect and everything that Israel does is pure and holy, there have been mistakes, aberrations and bad decisions over time but the favour, blessing and honour of God rests uniquely upon this nation as a model to all nations and that needs to be taken very seriously. b) God is most certainly not finished with them yet. He is still dealing with them strategically and practically and they are moving inexorably toward the pinnacle of their nationhood. The culmination of their journeys and learning, their final most glorious hours of history, their establishment as a blessed and pivotal people modelling nationhood to the world and preparing for the return of King Jesus to Jerusalem. c) Their size bears no relationship to their worth or effectiveness before God and toward the other peoples of the earth. Israel is one of the most significant nations on earth and for its size is such a profound influence and blessing to the world at large. And finally, d) God has decreed a powerful blessing to those who will pray for and work toward the peace of Israel and bless, honour and protect them as a nation and a people. This single, unique, particular and powerful blessing has immense capability to bring a quantum increase in the *genuine peace*, favour, protection and provision which each will experience in our lives. Its operation is effective at every level of society bringing blessing to whoever will pray for and bless Israel. On the contrary if one were to curse Israel, attack, damage or seek to destroy them, they will be cursed by God himself. The blessing or cursing of Israel is one of the most profoundly potent factors which will directly and exponentially affect the level of *genuine peace* in our lives, and throughout our nations. There is also a line of thought and research that the global diasporas and the migrations of Israel and her 'lost' tribes over the centuries have helped form the foundations of many of the western brotherhood of nations and that this is another way in which this tiny nation has been a blessing to the whole earth.

Israel also has a lot to teach the church...

The Church -is similar to Israel in that the followers and disciples of the Lord Jesus Christ are the ones who have heard the good news of the redemption of His cross, and salvation from sin and now seek to share it with others all over the world. And as each one accepts the Lord Jesus personally, they are adopted into the family of God, and as it were, into the nation and people of Israel, the chosen ones, with all the blessings and privilege which go along with that state. Some false beliefs regarding the church which serve to affect the level of peace in our world are a) Some are of the view that the gospel is not true and is based only on ancient mythology b) Others feel the message of the Christian church is irrational and too hard to understand c) Occasionally one finds the view that its message and principles are irrelevant to society and that it holds no real answers d) Particularly in the United States, there is a belief that one must separate church and state so as not to unduly influence citizens with the Gospel e) There is also an element who believe that the church is in a state of disarray, disunity and disagreement and suffers with low self-esteem or even self-hate f) A few would even say that Christians are easy lovers, soft touches, pushovers, suckers for a good sob story, bleeding hearts. That they are all love, with no boundaries, no common sense, allowing others to take advantage, lacking in discipline, and not interested in strategic action, to deal with root causes, in order to achieve permanent positive change g) Some would even suggest they are impotent, lacking power and courage, soft and weak, with no real ability to change the world for the better. That they are just doing first aid patch ups and temporary fixes to the world's problems. h) Finally, they are also occasionally accused of being what I call blind pacifists, peace at any price people, who will whitewash over the issues, superficially placate warring parties and opposing opinions.

While in some circumstances and in individual cases there can be some truth to these statements, they are in the main totally and radically wrong, and holding on to such false beliefs is doing immeasurable damage to our world. Let's explore each issue for just a moment. a) Firstly, the Gospel of the Lord Jesus Christ is profoundly true and there is more evidence and firsthand testimony of its truth and veracity than any other set of circumstances, belief system, historical events or way of life that has ever occurred or existed in our world. The Judeo-Christian way contains all of the major principles required to make this world a place of *genuine peace*. We would see a radical improvement in our society's peace, harmony and prosperity, if we allowed the church and the principles of the Judeo-Christian way to assimilate fully into our general way of life. b) If one is really committed to seeking the truth contained in this way of life, its founding documents and faithful adherents, we would find that it makes great sense and is easy to understand. The confusion usually only comes when one is half-hearted, critical, negative or insincere. God seems to know when we are genuine, and His Holy Spirit will always help and guide genuine seekers. A natural, Godly and *genuine peace* will then begin to emerge in our lives as we seriously begin to immerse ourselves in the faith. c) Even though I often hear this false belief espoused, that the gospel is irrelevant, I don't really understand why. Jesus' way is deeply, pervasively and practically relevant, having something helpful to say about nearly every aspect of life. On those things where it appears to be silent, one can usually infer, reason or extrapolate from principles and examples which have been mentioned, together with the literal guidance of the Holy Spirit, which is always available to the children of God, clear ideas about how they might apply in other circumstances. I site the case of the books of Proverbs and Psalms in the Bible as clear examples of practical earthly and heavenly wisdom which when applied faithfully will lead to pervasive peace, both personal and corporate. d) The separation of church and state of which the Americans speak is a flawed concept based upon false premises and assumptions. The founding fathers where simply seeking to ensure there was no single state sponsored church which was given special favours, and that the 'secular' systems of the world would not pollute the values of the church, as well as ensuring that the country was not run by the church organization itself. It was certainly not meant to deny Christians or Christianity a presence in the marketplace. To be actively engaged in the marketplace is one of the things we are commanded to do as followers of Jesus. He knew that staying aloof from the marketplace would destroy society, which current western experiences are demonstrating. Yet the tide of understanding on this issue is beginning to turn. Removing the church from the marketplace is one of the key goals of communism and this approach has been shown to have failed radically, denying any vestige of *genuine peace* and hope for their societies. The ideal is for laws of the land to remain as consistent as possible with ecclesiastical (Biblical) principles and values in order to maximize *genuine peace*. And where these laws might be allowed to differ, it would normally be expected that biblical law would maintain the higher moral standard, and laws of the land should therefore never be allowed to over-ride these higher principles. e) The belief that the church is divided and in disarray and that Christians suffer with a low self-image is equally flawed. While there are differences between streams of Christianity about which we have contended over the years, the heart of the faith is strong and consistent, and even though we debate liberally with each other on many issues, when we have a common cause or are threatened by a common enemy we fall quickly into line and are ready for galvanized action with awesome effect. Furthermore, some often mistake Christian love, gentleness and humility for weakness and low self-image. This could not be further from the truth. Followers of the Lord Jesus are called sons and daughters of the One True and Living God for good reason. While they are typically by nature gentle, loving, wise and caring, they also operate at His behest, under His absolute authority and in His great and infinite power. They are awesome, compassionate, wise and devastatingly capable warriors. And finally, f) while some Christians do operate with soft love only, no expected or implied boundaries, skills transfer, education or accountability and not addressing the real root causes and issues... most in fact do not, and this is not a proper interpretation of Jesus' agape love. Most people who operate in this fashion are either young in the faith or misinformed on some of its key principles. It is every church's responsibility to teach their adherents all the foundational aspects of the faith and encourage maturity, wisdom and effectiveness in their lives.

However...
It is problematic to try to allow for multi-faith...
Multi-faith - The issues regarding seeking peace within multi-faith situations are in principle the same as for race and nations above.

Multi-culture - The issues for seeking peace within multi-culture situations are in principle the same as for race and nations above.

Now, to the workplace, it is a large part of everyone's life...
Work/Vocation - Work can and should be one of the most satisfying elements of a healthy and balanced life, and we all spend a significant portion of our lives in the workplace. So, in order to enjoy any level of *genuine peace* in our daily lives we need to achieve

substantial peace where we work. Some of the false beliefs which inhibit our ability to enjoy peace in the workplace are: a) The idea that work is a chore or a punishment from God and not to be enjoyed, somewhat like a prison sentence b) That we shouldn't have to work, the world owes us a living, let's not bother to do a good job and find excuses not to work at our best, or better still, refuse to work at all c) And then there is the general untruth that 'The Man' always takes advantage of us workers, so let's do everything we can to 'stick it to' business owners, employers, and managers, and make their lives and business as difficult as possible. Or alternatively d) Work is everything. It gives me meaning and purpose and makes me feel like 'somebody'. And finally, e) I must compete and progress at work, get promotions, pay rises, bigger job titles, fringe benefits, accolades, bonuses, status and recognition in order to feel I'm succeeding as a person.

These false beliefs are all very different one from the other, yet if we genuinely believe any one of them is true, we will inevitably behave in ways which will potentially cause ourselves undue stress, tension, misunderstandings, lack of job satisfaction, and ultimately create unhealthy relationships and conflict with workmates and bosses, spoiling their work enjoyment as well.

Consider the following. a) If we really believed work was a chore or punishment it would be extremely difficult for us to enjoy the experience, and neither would anyone else in our workplace, thus destroying our peace. The truth is that work is a privilege and blessing and is meant to be therapeutic, productive, satisfying, fulfilling and enjoyable, a gift from God himself and part of His perfect plan, as we humans team together to provide goods and services which are necessary and beneficial for humankind. We also typically learn to build sound relationships, acquire important life skills, and receive financial reward to spend on ourselves, our families and loved ones, as well as achieving numerous other positive and benevolent outcomes. Regarding b) which spurns the concept of work, most of the above reasoning also applies in principle. Furthermore, this false belief, while being totally unworkable in any society, in that if we don't work, technically we won't usually have food, lodging or basic needs for life, and this is not desirable for the wellbeing of the individual or the community. Providing welfare for someone who is unwilling to work is also not a norm in most societies, nor is it a human right. It is a benevolent privilege in some nations, which if it were to become routine, would create all sorts of selfish behaviour and an entitlement mentality, which can spoil a person's self-esteem, expectations, values and attitude to life. It is a Biblical principle that we should work in order to eat. This type of entitlement attitude causes conflicts and tensions, among individuals as well as negatively affecting those who have to work extra hard to provide the necessary resources to accommodate the needs or wants of those individuals who refuse to work. The truth is that work is the norm, should be expected of all of us, and when approached with a positive attitude gives us a great deal of satisfaction and enjoyment, as well as a sense of value and strong self-esteem. Even those of us with disabilities benefit when able to work to the level at which we are capable. And for c) if we truly believed that everyone was out to get us and take advantage of us, we would never have *genuine peace*. We would always suspect that bosses and owners have hidden and often negative agendas, to take advantage of us every chance they get. This could and often does, cause us to be suspicious, confrontational, self-protective, ungrateful, and greedy for more. The truth is however, a majority of bosses and owners, even though they are seeking to make a profit and a good living, are inherently trying to do the right thing by all stakeholders and endeavour to create a productive and stable business environment. It is however right and proper to always maintain a healthy self interest in order to make sure we are receiving a fair deal. We should also be sure to conduct ourselves with professional values, justice and boundaries regarding what we are prepared to do with and for our bosses, how we will behave and expect to be treated in the workplace, and how we balance our work with all the other responsibilities we have in life. With an appropriate and mutually respectful, honest, transparent and pragmatic approach, a high level of peace and commercial effectiveness can be achieved. One secret is to put yourself in the other party's shoes, consider all the relevant facts and issues and seek to work harmoniously and collaboratively to achieve ideal outcomes in all areas. Now d) is something very different. The core of this false belief is that we achieve our significance, value and worth from and through the work we do. Not only is this incorrect it is potentially soul destroying, allowing us to be opened up to all sorts of disadvantage. If we seek to draw our value and self-worth from the work that we do, our sense of peace, enjoyment and fulfilment in life is immediately put at risk and will depend entirely upon the unpredictable and uncontrollable elements of our particular vocation. Jobs and businesses are becoming some of the most uncertain and volatile elements of our daily lives. We are at the mercy and uncertainty of economy, government, unions, business, technological advancement, competition, invention, innovation, personal health, accidents, broken relationships, the supernatural, Divine interventions and so on. These are all things over which we usually have little or no control. We can lose our job at any time, governments can change, a business can fail, jobs can be made obsolete, priorities change, projects fail or are shutdown, budgets cut, accidents happen, health can fail, or we could be dead tomorrow. And there will always be another person available to step up and take our place. No one is indispensable. The bottom line is that most normal occupations in a commercial world have no enduring eternal benefit, worth or impact. The only areas from which we can truly draw genuine value and worth are those which are outside of, and go beyond, ourselves. The paramount example is our relationship with our Heavenly Father. The Lord Jesus Christ is the One True and Living God who exists beyond ourself, and our experiences of life. Through our relationship with Him and our accepting and embracing His redemption on the Cross, the flow on effect extends into every area of life and on into eternity. This true worth and ultimate value comes from the confidence, joy, peace, hope, love and security of an eternal and personal relationship with God in heaven. He is then also available and delighted to guide, enable and assist us in this life and position us for eternity with Him in heaven in the next stage of our existence. There are many other worthwhile things here in this life like a wonderful marriage, lifelong friendships, children, grandchildren and great grandchildren, the joy of a common cause which improves the lot of humankind, defends the innocent, overcomes evil and so on. But nothing compares with our personal relationship with our Loving God and Father who loves us beyond our ability to understand. And finally, e) there is the belief that we must compete aggressively and determinedly, in order to succeed, receive promotions and prosper in life. On the contrary, if everyone operated in this way in life, the working world and other community organisations and initiatives would be in a constant state of intensely stressful, striving, competition and chaos. 'Dog eat dog' as some would say, and there would never be any *genuine peace* in the workplace. The truth regarding this belief, is that when we are recognized, loved, honoured, blessed, encouraged and known intimately and personally by God himself, as well as ideally our spouses, children, friends and colleagues in a good and Godly common cause, we will not need the accolades, promotions and rewards of hectic careers, in order to feel valued and at peace. Instead, we will have a beautiful sense of satisfaction, joy and fulfilment in who we are, and with whom we are in relationship... and we will learn to be content and work with whatever level of blessings we receive... as we faithfully pursue life and vocation.

Leadership and Teaming - Leadership is a concept which has been studied and debated for thousands of years and is extremely important to the effectiveness of any society. It is important to note that anything which is too large for one person to do in this world requires leadership and teaming in order to operate efficiently and achieve worthwhile and quality results. Poor leadership and teaming creates endless conflict, while good leadership and effective teams are efficient, a pleasure to watch, and to work in and with. It goes without saying that a strong level of *genuine peace* will always be evident in an effective team with quality leadership. It should also be noted for further reference that effective team leadership has been explored in various detail in my earlier books. Now here are some false beliefs which will always serve to inhibit or destroy the peace and effectiveness of human teams. Firstly, comes the untruth that leadership is a) lording it over people, making them do what you want them to do, the way you want them to do it. While on the surface this sounds rational and logical, it is in fact false. No sensible balanced human being enjoys working in a situation where they are just treated like machines or slaves, being forced and expected to do exactly what they are told, without question, comment, feedback understanding or room for creativity or flexibility. It is soul destroying. A good leader will typically share their strategy, objectives, thinking and intentions with the goal of seeking buy-in and a unified well-informed resolve from and with team members. When this works well it produces profoundly effective results and should difficulties arise requiring changes to be made etc., the strong level of openness transparency and trust serves to foster maximum flexibility, responsiveness, creativity and efficiency. The next false belief is that leadership is b) taking advantage of people, being manipulative, deceptive and treating them as just pawns in your game, to achieve your own ends, or that of someone else, without any thought for the individual's personal needs. This is wrong in a thousand different ways. It is a blatant and often wilful defiance of the eternal and Divine instruction to 'love your neighbour' and 'do unto others as you would have them do unto you'. Sadly, this type of behaviour is always eventually destructive to the perpetrator and incurs the natural repercussions of rebellious opposition to the good and righteous ways of God Himself. It is not a healthy place for any human-being to walk. Any natural, or should I say supernatural, heavenly blessing which flows routinely from walking in the positive and perfect will of our Loving Heavenly Father is thwarted or negated. Worse still the individual also incurs a non-blessing or un-blessing which is a direct result of moving themselves out of the place of obedience and God's blessing. To make the matter even more miserable, people who operate in this negative way toward others and the world around them, become fair game for the enemy of God who seeks to kill, steal and destroy all that is good. Satan and his minions become immediately aware that the person has lost the blessing and covering of God, because of what they have done or not done, and they are fully exposed, at the mercy as it were, of those beings who themselves have no mercy. The dark hordes then have opportunity, according to the Laws of God's universe, to harass the perpetrators to their hearts content. And God will then typically not intervene until He is asked to or senses an attitude of repentance or a potential change of heart. It is also important to note that in the interest of working toward a broad-based *genuine peace* across all of society, if we should happen to be working for a boss of this type, we need to have the courage to speak out and do or say something about it. This will disturb the peace initially but hopefully will cause a sequence of events that should ultimately lead to resolution of the problem. For example, challenging the boss on bad behaviour, and maybe even intending to resign or report the situation if the negative behaviour doesn't change, would cause tension. However, if enough people were to do this the 'bad' boss would hopefully get the message and change behaviour, or alternatively, eventually no one would want to work in that business, and would choose not to do so, thus causing the business to fail. On the contrary treating your employees fairly and justly will help the business to flourish. These types of situations can sometimes be very complicated, and one should ideally seek the advice of wise, mature, trusted individuals with appropriate skill and experience in the required area. It's also important to reflect, analyse, pray and consider the implications of taking remedial action, as well as the desirability and manageability of possible outcomes, before initiating the process, in order to maximise chances of success and minimize any potentially negative flow-on effects. Another false belief which steals the peace of the marketplace is c) that it is good to micro-manage your people in every aspect of their job. This generally does not work either, since most people do not appreciate someone looking over their shoulder all of the time. It often causes feelings ranging from mild discomfort or insecurity to that of feeling massively crowded, stressed, frustrated, annoyed, and experiencing a sense of being 'watched' and not trusted. Such supervisory behaviour usually causes disharmony in the workplace and often increases incidence of 'bad blood' in relationships and increased errors on the job. Of course, it's ok to work closely with employees who are learning a new task, but only for a short time with the emphasis on mastering the new skill in a timely manner, then being trusted to deliver results with only occasional supervisory check-in to ensure that all is going well. Otherwise, people should be given room to move and a sense of pride and ownership in what they are being asked to do. This increases enjoyment and satisfaction. Workers should have just the right level of instruction, commensurate with their skill and experience levels, and then allowed to enjoy themselves and be creative within the bounds of delivering what they are asked for in a timely, productive and quality fashion. Then there is the myth that d) criticising people and putting them down in public for mistakes or misdemeanours and such, actually keeps them 'on their toes' and highly productive. Nothing could be further from the truth. Human beings need encouragement, and constant criticism eventually demoralises, smothers, crushes, damages or even kills the human spirit. Such behaviour very soon destroys camaraderie and productivity. On the contrary, wise, sincere, open, honest, compassionate, constructive correction and encouragement are the greatest motivation and effectiveness enhancing aids of all time. And here is another classic. Some people believe that it's good to tell workers only the most minimal information about the task at hand, and thus e) 'keeping them in the dark' regarding other project, team and job goals, objectives and rationale.

This strategy is flawed in that it reduces enjoyment of the workers because there is no sense of being part of something larger, which they understand and are invested in. Such leadership behaviour usually increases the risk of error and reduces overall quality, effectiveness and job satisfaction. However, when a team is fully informed regarding what they are aiming for as an overall goal and fully understand their part in the process and how it all fits together they will inevitably enjoy what they are doing and produce a much better quality result. And finally continuing on from above, some believe f) that one does not need to give positive motivation, reward or recognition. That people should just do what is expected of them in order to earn their wages. As previously stated, and seemingly obvious, all human beings need to be encouraged, rewarded and recognized in order to feel fulfilled, successful, joyful and at peace.

Now Sadly, I have no more space to further develop these ideas. There are certainly many other categories of **false beliefs** which are inhibiting *genuine peace* in our society, so I have included the remaining summarized information from my research. Please reflect at your leisure with the goal of articulating solutions to the stated false beliefs in the hearts and minds of ourselves and others, so that we might continue to enhance the levels of *genuine peace* in our world.

Education and Learning –
False Beliefs:-
a) Education is the answer to everything and will make me smarter and richer

b) We can trust the world's 'secular' systems, teachers and philosophers to educate our children
c) Academia is everything, and knowledge learned by hands-on apprenticeship or being an understudy in the workplace is inferior
d) There is only one way to learn, that is by words and instruction
e) I don't need to learn, I already know everything I need to know
f) We should just keep learning for the sake of knowledge and information itself and the pride and satisfaction of being knowledgeable
g) It doesn't matter who we learn from, all knowledge is beneficial. Knowledge doesn't have to be given within a real worldview context but can be absorbed and assimilated within a values vacuum
h) Knowledge doesn't have to have practical application to real life, esoteric is fine
i) We don't need to be taught what is right and wrong. It's all relative anyway and each person can work it out for themselves
j) If we have more education, it makes us better than those who have less
k) We don't need to learn the basics, computers and robots will do it for us

Words and Language –
False Beliefs:-
a) Words and language are not important
b) Spelling and grammar are unimportant
c) The meanings of words are not very important
d) We don't need to bother to learn English well and make sure we are careful to articulate things properly and well

e) How people interpret what I say doesn't really matter. That's their problem, why should I care
f) It doesn't matter if I can't understand the words of others
g) It doesn't matter if the words or phrases of others affect my spirit by evoking negative, positive or destructive emotions
h) I am not easily led by the words of others

Literature –

False Beliefs:-

a) I don't need to read what other people say
b) It doesn't matter what type of books I read
c) Reading books keeps me from doing real stuff
d) I should not have to read stuffy old classics from generations ago
e) Books are out of date and parse now, with the advent of internet, blogs and such
f) A good movie is better than a book

Ideas, Dreams and Visions –

False Beliefs:-

a) Ideas, dreams and visions are of no value; they are esoteric, abstract and of no physical substance
b) They are the domain of 'day-dreamers', 'navel-gazers' and 'gunnas' who imagine and reflect on many things but never get anything done
c) They are usually inspired by wrong motives, obsessions, cravings, negative spirits and such and can lead one astray toward impossible goals and non-productive outcomes

Growing and Maturing –

False Beliefs:-

a) It's not worth seeking to grow in wisdom, life skills and maturity because then you just become capable of more, and more will be expected of you
b) Responsibility is a real burden and chore, and why should one bother when nobody else seems to care or make an effort
c) Anyway, it's all too hard. The world is in such a mess that there is no chance of making a difference, so why should we try
d) There is no personal strategic benefit in being mature and responsible in life, always seeking to be a positive example, and doing that which is wise and right and good

Media –
False Beliefs:-
a) You can trust the media to do and say the right thing
b) Media and journalists will always seek and report the truth without fear or favour
c) Media and journalists can always deliver messages without bias
d) Media is always a valuable and critically important element to a peaceful society
e) Social networking is always a reliable and beneficial form of media, allowing information to be reliably shared by an infinite number of alternate individuals and channels in a plethora of different ways
f) Google-like internet based integrated repositories of information are a fully reliable trustworthy form of knowledge media for a peaceful society
g) Media is a satisfactory alternative to honest, open, transparent, truth-based, well-informed

communications through networks of quality, trusted, committed, human relationships

Military –

False Beliefs:-

a) Military action or war should never be necessary in order to solve problems
b) Taking military action is always morally wrong
c) A nation should not need an army or other standing military force in order to defend and protect its citizens and way of life) Anything goes in war time and there is no action which cannot be justified
d) You can allow any national, cultural, political or philosophical individuals to join your national military
e) You can trust the military and do not need rules of war or limits to authority

Government –

False Beliefs:-

a) Government should do everything, provide everything and be everything to everybody
b) Democracy is the perfect form of government and will work in every situation
c) It doesn't matter who you have running the country because if they do a bad job, you can just vote them out
d) Government needs to make a rule for everything, so citizens know what to do and not do
e) Governments can or should treat all cultures, value systems and world views as equal and allow them all to proliferate in the nation
f) Government representatives have to do what the individuals, minorities and masses of people whom

they govern want them to do
g) National governments must surrender their sovereignty to a Global Government/Entity

Business –
False Beliefs:-
a) Business is an evil endeavour and shouldn't be encouraged in society
b) Business takes advantage of its suppliers, customers and staff) All business people are basically greedy and/or corrupt
c) Business activities cannot be effectively regulated to do the right thing
d) Big businesses should not be allowed to make big profits, we should tax away all their profits
e) Government could and should do all the commerce that is needed, there is no need for private enterprise
f) Most community needs could be provided by small cottage or farming based entities
g) Countries do not need to manufacture or create all their own basic needs, any gaps can be fulfilled by trade with neighbouring countries

Arts –
False Beliefs:-
a) All art is positive and beneficial
b) We should encourage all forms of art in our society
c) We should allow artists to create whatever they choose without censorship or direction
d) We should allow artists to create their art wherever they choose without constraints
e) Artists should all be allowed to live on welfare in the interests of supporting their craft

And so on...

I trust consideration of these examples has demonstrated some of the ways in which beliefs can and do affect the quality and peacefulness of our lives and has helped to show that a major key to achieving *genuine peace* is to hold onto and live by beliefs which are based on truth. I pray this has been helpful and will encourage further reflection and additional research on topics of personal or corporate need or interest.

Chapter 8 - Inner Brokenness Inhibits True Peace

I am blessed to have lived a long and fulfilling life with myriad varieties of learning opportunities across a broad span of topics. I have read, researched, studied, catalogued and experienced first and second hand, all manner and forms of 'brokenness' which we human beings can experience. This topic is also worthy of a book in its own right, and many have already been written, as well as some excellent training and counselling material. My objective here however is simply to bring a high-level summary list of some of the key 'brokenness' issues which will often inhibit our corporate and personal peace. Some of these have been alluded to earlier in this book. Once again for simplicity and space economy I will just list the items and suggest a brief 'one liner' approach as to how they may be addressed in our own personal lives.

The topics are for example:-

Negative Father figure issues. The secret here is to counter these by seeking out and discovering who God really is, His wonderful, loving, affirming, supportive nature and entering in to a close and personal relationship with Him to compensate for any earthly experiences with inadequate or inappropriate fathering. Often, we will need help with this. But I have seen miraculous life changes in this area once we realize who God really is and how deeply He loves us.

Negative Mother figure issues. As with father issues stated above, God also has the ability to compensate for inadequate mothering, if we will surrender ourselves to this open and loving heavenly relationship, which is made possible through the agency and redemptive power of the cross of the Lord Jesus Christ.

Orphan spirit, abandonment, rejection, low self-esteem, and insecurity. Solution is to study the Bible looking for references as to how God sees us generally and also to ask Him how He sees you personally and specifically. You being His son or daughter, and then accept that no matter what our earthly situation is, we are adopted into the family of God, and have all the attributes of royalty and privilege available to us, and all the benefits and promises which go along with that. I encourage you to read His book regularly and with passion and an open heart. He will speak words of healing that will comfort and restore your soul. Speak to Him about it and watch how your heart and perspectives begin to change.

Inability or unwillingness to hear the voice of God. God is always speaking and if we will reach out to Him in humility, with a willingness to surrender our lives and walk in obedience to His heavenly way, He will make himself heard inside our heart, thoughts and circumstances. All we need to do then is take action on the things He shares with us, and we will never be the same again. If you've never done so before, why not ask Him now. I assure you that you will be delighted, and a whole new level of enlightenment will begin to unfold in your life.

Knowing what God wants for us but being unwilling to follow His lead. This is a tricky one, because it is a form of rebelliousness against God. Disobeying what we know God wants of us puts us in a difficult position and denies us the blessings which He intends for us. It's like thumbing our nose at God and saying we know better. It's everyone's choice of course, but I know that if someone you know struggles with this, choosing God's way is always the most wonderful, satisfying fulfilling way of all, even though it may be a bit scary to begin with...

Feeling a sense of guilt or shame. Usually caused by sin we have committed in our lives or the fact that we find ourselves in modest, meagre, difficult, or embarrassing circumstances. It can even be caused when we have persistently been falsely accused, attacked, demeaned, mocked, blamed or put down by authority figures or someone who didn't love us tenderly and encourage us on the journey of life. This can also sow brokenness in our heart. The answer here is also discovering that we are sons and daughters of God through acceptance of Jesus redemptive act on the cross and that we therefore have access to all the spiritual blessings of heaven and the Divine potential to change our circumstances. It means for example whenever we feel shame or embarrassment, give it to Jesus, He's promised to take it so we don't have to bear it anymore. We are free, our accuser was defeated on the cross. On occasions there can also be a form of demonically inspired false shame/guilt which if not released by the above processes may need some help through deliverance.

Feeling that we need to perform and achieve a high standard in order to be loved, accepted and worthwhile. Sometimes this is caused by poor or unduly strict, rigid, unfair, inconsistent, illogical or irrational parenting or leadership behaviour by one or more authority figures in our life. They may have put us down, spoke negatively about our work at the time or of achievements generally. There may have been a personality conflict where we never felt up to the mark because we were told we were bad, or different, didn't do it right, didn't achieve the set task as requested, did not get a high enough standard and so on. This can cause us to consciously or unconsciously strive and feel pressure to perform to a sometimes inordinately high standard, socially, emotionally, economically, spiritually, mentally, morally and practically, in behaviour, image management or reputation, at school, work, play, sport or even how we dress, the car we drive, the places we go, where we volunteer etc. This can easily become a very real and very distressing, debilitating issue in life. Always being concerned that we have to perhaps live up to a certain standard and often being embarrassed or ashamed because we feel we haven't, in our own eyes or in those whom we like to please or impress. Worse still there can be those with whom we will never be allowed to look good, because of ill-will, jealously or bad- hearted relationships toward us. The secret is once again to see ourselves as God sees us in Christ and know that we are loved no matter what we've done or not done, or the standard to which we have performed. Yes, Father God does want us to be and to do the very best we can, but he knows our heart, circumstances, resource constraints, personal challenges, and fully understands that while we walk this earth, we will never be perfect. He does and will always love and affirm us no matter what we do or don't do, He will never withdraw that love and He is always available to help us with any issues we may be facing. We are so precious to Him that I cannot adequately put it into words. As long as our heart is toward Him and we desire to follow Jesus with integrity, using what we have and who we are, He is always for us and never against us. He is always speaking highly of us in heaven and on earth. Even before we give our hearts to Him, He still loves, affirms and celebrates who we are, how He made us and the amazing gifts and talents that we have. He also gently and deftly shows us our sin and leads us to practice repentance so we can remain in His perfect will. He knows His plans for us, and they are good plans, plans for a hope and a future, plans to bless and not to curse. He is always ready to help us be who we are meant to be and achieve what we are meant do. And that is always enough for Daddy God. Even when we are struggling, He understands and is there to help and walk with us. We can be totally free of this performance trap. With the help of Jesus and loving mentors and friends, we can reframe how we see the world and even though we seek to perform well, we will never have to be concerned about what others may or may not think about us. It only really matters what God feels or says about us. When working in earthly teams for example, we will naturally need to be submitted to each other and walk in humility and mutual consideration seeking to help the team succeed, but our highest objective will always be to keep on track with Father God's overall higher purpose agenda. He will always ensure that any important earthly objectives are achieved but without the inordinate pressure to 'perform'. If we are walking in His ways, close to His heart, slowly the number of people with unrealistic expectations or unfair and unloving observations and judgments on us will reduce significantly, maybe even disappear out of our lives. But nevertheless, we can be free of being concerned about what others may think.

Hurts on the journey of life. Often incurred through no fault of our own, this can cause us to feel bruised, broken, demoralized, debilitated, depressed, frustrated, trapped, angry, violent and such. Once again this is not a hopeless situation and with a right relationship with God, and our brother and sister followers of the Lord Jesus, we can be completely healed and have victory over all of these things. It requires willingness to surrender, an experience of receiving Christ and being born again into Him, and then an infilling of His Holy Spirit. It is also critical for us to 'let go' of the people who have hurt us and leave any punishment they might need or deserve up to God, who judges all righteously and fairly. This will then allow us to enter into a positive new mindset, a new worldview which actually makes sense and really works, and an amazing new way of thinking, feeling and acting, which maximizes enjoyment and fulfillment in life, while not being limited by what people may have said or done to us in the past.

Taking offence. This is when we allow something that is said or done to lodge in our heart, do us damage, and cause us to react with strong negative emotions. It can sometimes feel involuntary or even 'normal' yet is usually a residual behaviour pattern resulting from a negative memory or event, an injury, abuse, a belief which is untrue, an ineffective method of processing information, an inner vow, a strong, rigid or unrealistic expectation and so forth. Some people call this 'being triggered' or hitting a 'hot button'. Taking offence destroys peace and makes it difficult to re-establish, but the bottom line is that how we react or respond is always within our control, and a choice we can make with the help of God. One way to address this problem is to take the words or actions as they come and capture them, metaphorically speaking, in 'mid-air', holding them outside of ourselves like a shield or force-field would... Then while we are holding them 'out there'; consider them objectively and thoughtfully with an 'unbroken' mindset as described above. Take note of what and why we think this may have happened. Ask God's advice about what they meant, what to do about it, and how to deal with the matter appropriately. But do not take it into our spirit, mind or heart, until the situation is fully processed 'out there' away from our vital parts. Only the fully processed outcomes, thoughts and ideas should be constructively and lovingly acted upon. For example, to pray for the one who 'threw' them at You, that they might find God themselves, process whatever pain or demon caused them to do it, and ultimately change their behaviour... and indeed we need to also make any positive changes in our own lives, which seem necessary as a result of the interaction and discernment we have just experienced. This re-imagining of our world in Christ Jesus will do wonders as we allow the redemptive power of His cross to change and heal our hearts and redefine how we process what others say and do to us personally. Sometimes however, taking offence is deeply entrenched, compulsive, endemic and demonically driven to the point where we may need assistance through deliverance as well.

Un-forgiveness - Occurs when someone hurts us and we refuse to release them into God's hands for judging. We want to hold them guilty and judge them accordingly ourselves. The solution is to forgive them and release them into God's hands immediately, or if we are having difficulty doing that, for example, due to the horrific nature of what they may have perpetrated upon us, and the trauma which is still lodged in our soul, we could do the following:- ask God to open their eyes to the grievance they have done, ask Him to deal with it accordingly, ask Him to release us from the pain and trauma we have experienced, and help us to bless, rather than curse, and to pray for their healing etc. Eventually we will arrive at a point of forgiveness and an ability to release them to God for mercy or judgment, and we ourselves will then be set free from any residual issues and effects. We also need to realize that some people are not interested in Godliness and may be walking in wilful wickedness, bound demonically, and will purposely cause grief wherever they go. When we have this type of person in our lives, we need to ensure we are not a victim to their sin. We need to give up our assumed 'right' to respond negatively to them, set strong positive boundaries to protect our vital parts, keep them at a safe distance, intercede for their salvation when we are able, and move on past the current difficult situation leaving it in God's hands. Hopefully one day they will have a change of heart.

Being judgmental, critical and condemnatory. This is often related to un- forgiveness above. The solution is the same, but to help us reach healing we often need to ask ourselves why we have chosen to sit in a place of judgment upon the other party and ask God for His understanding as to why this is so, and what we need to do in order to be released. It's not a good place to put ourselves, because God's laws of the universe cause the way in which we judge others to ultimately be visited upon us. This is not a good place to sit. It steals our peace and can even damn our eternal soul.

Holding onto negative inner vows and nurturing a heart of stone. Solutions are as for un-forgiveness and being judgmental above. We often harbor these vows because of past hurts, and we need to revisit, reanalyse, rethink, reprocess, and reinvent the way we interpret the negative event, and reconfigure the way we store it in our memory. This needs to be done in the light of God's mercy and grace, and a renewed, pure and completely healed heart, which we have achieved by entering fully into the above experiences and learning. We also need to learn how to set wholesome boundaries around our relationships and interactions with others to minimize the chances of it happening again, and to avoid the risk of making any more unhelpful negative vows in the future. An example of one of these would be the attitude of hardness of heart in saying that 'I hate all men' because of what he/they have done to me. Furthermore, so that they may never be able to do it again, I vow to never ever trust them or allow them to get close to me again. These types of vow have the effect of warping, corrupting and polluting how we see the world, and how we read circumstances and events which happen in life. It is so wonderful to be free of such vows, or at least to have much less of them in our lives, so we can see things as they really are, interpret them more accurately and respond more appropriately. Rather than reacting out of a slightly warped worldview. Identifying and dealing with these issues, brings much more peace into our hearts and minds and reduces stresses on those around us as well, thus contributing significantly to *genuine peace*. It also allows us to begin softening our hearts and taking more risks with reaching out, connecting and doing life with others.

Not leveraging the fullness of the Gospel of Jesus Salvation. The salvation of the Lord Jesus Christ is such a multifaceted, total and complete reinvention of who we are, how we feel, how we see the world around us and how we interact with others, that it impacts every area of our body, soul and spirit. It also by its very nature has the potential to vitally and positively affect the world around us. We need to enter in to all the fullness of this salvation in order to experience *genuine peace*, and a majority of the world need to do so as well. That is why the Judeo-Christian faith needs to be spread across the entire world. It is the only environment where this genuine healing can be found and from which it can be propagated.

The inability to be a strong conduit of God's agape love. My entire third book 'Learning Places: Real Love' is dedicated to this subject. It comes as a result of the salvation spoken of above and is required to be in operation across the entire world, with the majority of people practicing this love, if we are ever to achieve *genuine peace*. I've also previously reiterated that this selfless, others- seeking love, which always wants the best for the other party, especially that they might connect in a strong relationship with God, know themselves fully, become fully healed, and be able to love others in the world around them... needs to be broadly applicable across society in order to have maximum positive and peaceful effect. This is eminently possible for all of us. It just takes the will, commitment and determination to know God to the maximum, experience His healing, and to maintain passion by asking the Holy Spirit to enable us to make Him known to others, on every day, in every way. Remembering that when our hearts are not fully healed it is difficult for agape to flow through us to others.

The inability to experience the joys of koinonia body-life fellowship. This beautiful fellowship is the outworking of the above agape love and describes the type of relationship and interaction we are meant to have with each other in order to bring *genuine peace* into our world. One cannot have koinonia without agape and agape is not possible without salvation.

I trust that considering the different types of brokenness and how they inhibit true peace, has been helpful and will give insight into the inner healing that can potentially be experienced, by every man, woman and child in Christ Jesus.

Finally, in seeking to experience true koinonia that we will be able to see our way clear to appropriate this for ourselves fully... and then help others to do so as well. So that koinonia (which brings *genuine peace*) in all its richness, can be experienced, in every tribe and tongue and nation across the whole earth... until He comes.

Chapter 9 - Impact of Spiritual Oppression

Spiritual oppression is the action of demon spirits upon human beings with the intention of hurting us in body, soul and spirit, spoiling, destroying or weakening our relationship with God, and each with other, in marriages, families, friendships, communities, cities and nations. Anywhere and in every way possible they seek to stop the agency of God's Love and Salvation coming to this earth and achieving the *genuine peace* it is meant to bring.

There is much which could and has been said on this topic, but for the purposes of this book, I choose to simply mention the following.

The best that we can do is to enter into the fullness of salvation in the Lord Jesus Christ and become spiritually aware through daily reflective study of the Bible, and the agency of hearing the voice of God, directly through our personal relationship with Him. Then we will progressively become more fully aware of the activities of these demons, their strategies, tricks and campaigns and become a strong, unified, cohesive army to oppose them on every front. Until they eventually become exhausted and demoralized, because they lose every battle they dare to wage against we who are the sons and daughters of the One True and Living God, and brothers, soldiers, saints and priests with King Jesus.

Other tools we have in addition to general principles in the Bible, and specific instructions through prayer and devotional times with God, are the gifts of the Holy Spirit. These are word of wisdom, word of knowledge, faith, healings, miracles, prophecy, discernment, tongues and interpretation of tongues. Then there is the fruit of the Spirit; love, joy, peace, patience, kindness, goodness, faithfulness, gentleness and self control. All of these are powerful and effective agents in observing, discerning, deciding and taking action against spiritual oppression by demons and principalities, either directly or by way of other wilful or innocent human beings. It is important to reflect as well, that though demons are mostly invisible, you can almost assume that they are involved in some way directly or indirectly when chronic, deep seated, abhorrent behaviour, serious addictions or wilful sin is involved. And we don't need to worry or be fearful when people talk about demons. It's fair to say that they are just simply a fact of life and constantly trying to cause us to do new sin, hold us in existing sin, whether it is habitual or ad hoc, or alternatively trying to confuse, distract, misdirect, frustrate, discourage and demoralize us, to keep us from doing that which is needful, right and good. Rather than worrying about them as a concept, it is best to just resist them in Jesus Name, be rid of them and develop new more Godly, peaceful and satisfying habits and behaviour.

It should also be noted that our true enemies are not flesh and blood, but powers, spirits and principalities of the darkness. So, while still needing to hold appropriate boundaries with flesh and blood people who may seek to hurt us, we need to address the spirits within and around people. We also need to understand that God is the Sovereign God of the universe and has power and authority over all beings. Furthermore, He has delegated His authority to us in the earth to make disciples of all nations. This means that as we operate in relationship with God and according to His will, we have authority over demons which operate in the earth. When we resist them, they must flee. Free will is important here though. In relation to ourselves if we resist demons they will flee from us, but if we choose to continue to sin they will use this 'chink' in our armour to come back and continue to harass us. The same principle applies when praying for others. They must flee as we command in Jesus' Name but will seek to return if the person continues to allow them to, through wilful sin or playing with the things of darkness and not submitting all thoughts to the Lordship of Christ. Follow-up and ongoing accountability, moral support, friendship, prayer and mentoring are therefore often needed to help ensure that people maintain their healing and deliverance. It is also important that in order to operate in deliverance for our-selves, and while taking territory from the enemy or releasing others from demons, we need to operate in obedience and holiness at all times. However, once we are walking in a good place with God, walking in righteousness, abiding with Him in covenant relationship, loving God and man and obeying Him in all things, the demons are subject to us in Christ's Name. We are free to, and in fact commanded to, release people from them, and take our world back from the brink of darkness on all fronts, in all domains of society. Let's be diligent and passionate in this life-long campaign and redeem our nations and govern them for Him and according to His Way.

For completeness sake, it also needs to be noted that some people will inevitably love darkness rather than light and chaos instead of peace. This means that there will always be some who reject this path of *genuine peace* and depending on the degree of strife or issue they choose to take in this regard, will dictate the most peaceful, humane, constructive and effective way to deal with them. Sadly, some will need to be in prison, others on heavy medication and some will need to be institutionalized in order to protect their own personal safety and that of the community. It has always been thus, but there is always a free will choice and maximum opportunity for repentance, healing and recovery, through the name and power of the Lord Jesus Christ. Sadly, at the moment there seems to be so many more folk suffering in this place than needs to be, due to the unwillingness of 'powers that be' to seriously consider this Judeo-Christian *genuine peace* approach to healing, rehabilitation and recovery. I feel sure that when we 'turn the tide' and include these values in our daily lives and community culture again and encourage others to take advantage of them... That we will see miracles like serious reductions in prison and other institutional populations, along with massively reduced need for psychological care, drug policing and rehabilitation, family and community violence remediation etc. What a joy that will be.

Chapter 10 - A Viable Worldview is Critical as Well

Finally, let's explore the importance of worldview. Earlier in this book my research, analysis, thought processes and conclusions identified that for a nation to thoroughly prosper and enjoy an ideal way of life it needs to be established and governed according to Judeo-Christian principles and values. This chapter is a brief summary of this type of worldview and includes one liner examples of what that would typically entail.

A worldview is a big-picture perspective of what the world would look like operating according to a given set of values and beliefs. It can also be described as a way of perceiving the world around us. Ideal *genuine peace* occurs when the world is based upon a set of values and beliefs which actually have the capacity to engender a way of true peace, and when each citizen's expectations, view of the world and personal values are consistent with that nationally operating worldview.

This may sound like a lofty dream, even too good to be possible, but the thesis of this book and its final conclusions demonstrate clearly that this is in fact the only way we will ever achieve true peace in our world. Let's explore this type of ideal worldview and what it might look like.

A Judeo-Christian Worldview would seek to ensure:-
- The One True and Living God is honoured as creator and sustainer of all

- Freedom of religion is allowed in private but no other God to be worshipped in public places
- Temples and idols to other gods are not allowed to be created or visible in public places
- We recognize there is good and evil in the world. But as a society we choose only good
- There is also right and wrong, and truth and error. We choose truth and right
- God will be honoured with times and days for all to have rest and recreation
- Marriage is encouraged and is between one man and one woman, ideally for life
- Government and community support will assist our marriages to succeed
- Children are acknowledged to be best raised by their mother and father
- Fathers, mothers and families are to be honoured by children and the state
- Fostering and adoption into functional families will be the norm for orphans
- Single parents are to be honoured and assisted in their key role as seeking to make the best of a broken marriage by helping the children to survive and flourish as a unit without the benefit of both fulltime parents
- Second marriages are to be treated with the same seriousness and solemnity as first marriages with a view to commitment and longevity, and stepchildren are honoured and assisted to grow and flourish in the absence of one of the natural parents
- Humanity is considered to be steward of all creation on God's behalf
- Human beings are made in God's image and deemed of high worth and purpose

- Human Life is precious and to be preserved from conception to death
- All will be encouraged to find and fulfill their life purpose and destiny
- All are expected to act in Godly ways. e.g., Love God and love neighbour
- All are to live in harmony with each other consistent with this worldview
- Murder, theft, lying, bribery, corruption, kidnapping will all be illegal
- Paedophilia, blackmail, polygamy, bestiality will all be illegal
- Fornication, promiscuity, adultery would be strongly discouraged
- God is to be honoured and respected in all government processes
- All government legislation must be compliant with this worldview
- All media outlets and channels will conform to this worldview
- Media is free to discuss and debate this worldview but only truthfully
- Arts, sports, entertainment will conform to this worldview as for media
- Business and commerce will conform to this worldview and be honest and fair.
- Health industry will reaffirm and promote this worldview, value life and natural ideas
- The Lord Jesus Christ is celebrated as Saviour and Redeemer of the world
- All students are taught the principles of Biblical Judeo-Christianity at school
- Pre-school, primary, secondary and tertiary all adhere to this worldview

- All are encouraged to read and seek to live by Bible principles
- All are encouraged to seriously consider following the Jesus Way
- Defence, police, security, border control will all comply with this worldview
- The judiciary, judges, courts magistrates will all comply with this worldview
- Perjury will be illegal in all courts and formal institutions and tribunals
- Trial by Godly judges or a jury of peers when charge is serious, will be the norm
- Borders will be protected, and no illegal migrants or refugees will be received
- Foreign entrants must agree to conform to this worldview or be returned home

I think you can quickly see why, when implemented broadly and with integrity, wisdom and compassion, this way of life and worldview is desirable and positive, and a joy for all of its adherents, as well as all the other citizens who live within its purview.

Chapter 11 - How Do We Achieve This Wonderful Peace?

While seeking thoughts about how to wrap up this topic I was led to the book of First Peter, Chapter 4. Written by one of the great original apostles, it embodies some of his final words of advice and encouragement to the followers of Jesus, just before he left this earth for his heavenly home. He was a very experienced and practical man, a fisherman, and his thoughts ring of radical simplicity and profound wisdom. Let me paraphrase and extrapolate some of his thoughts in terms which are directly relevant to the core theme of this book.

Enduring peace is rarely achieved, without a series of intense battles to confront, engage, resist, overcome, process, refine and resolve, all of the issues going on between light and darkness, in order to bring about a new Divine order. This includes the marvellous miracle concept of *genuine peace*. Peter is suggesting that in order to reach this place, we need to be 'sold out for', 'all in with', 'totally abandoned to' and 'wholly committed toward' the cause of King Jesus. To be half-hearted in these volatile days just makes us vulnerable 'cannon-fodder' for the spiritual elements which seek to undermine, tear down and destroy our/His way of life. Alternatively, if we are fully engaged with King Jesus, he has an inexhaustible supply of heavenly resources available at His command to sustain, guide, direct, protect and give us ultimate success. But it is important to note that since He has given us free will, which we have typically abused, we first need to be personally involved with Jesus and the cross, in an attitude of repentance and submission, in order to receive redemption. We are then able and ready to engage with the broader campaign. It is also noteworthy that our eternal and all-powerful King also chooses, indeed often insists for our own personal development and perfecting toward His image, in using us individually and collectively to achieve many of these battle outcomes. However, He always prioritizes our protection, provision and guidance, and supports us in the campaign, to ensure that the wars are ultimately won by His righteous army. The first battle is our own inner, personal struggle, on the frontier of mind and heart, and once we have won that war, which we can only do with the help of God and trusted friends and brothers and sisters in Christ, we can then seek to help others win theirs. And in due course join our forces with other willing, righteous allies across the body of Christ to take larger and greater kingdom objectives.

God, our Heavenly Father, needs us to be highly trained and disciplined, fighting soldiers on assignment. We are to be clear-minded, self-controlled, prayerful, alert and powerful, spiritual warriors, like marines, navy seals or special servicemen. This means we have to turn our eyes and heart away from our past selfish, futile, frivolous, worthless, (even shameful) behaviour and focus all our physical and spiritual resources and energy into the King's campaign. One of our key goals here is to resist and repel darkness in all its forms, wherever we find it, and spread the good news about the redemption Jesus won for us on the cross. We are to help as many as will accept the gospel, to avoid the eternal judgment of God upon their lives. God does not want to judge men and women, but sin has to be dealt with, it cannot enter into Heaven, else there would be no peace and perfection there. And if we think we have no sin, we have been deceived and taken advantage of, and if we cling to unrighteousness, and stay attached to it indefinitely and it to us, we are doomed to end up where unrighteousness ends up. There is only one solution to this: the redemption of the Lord Jesus Christ. Once rid of sin and unrighteousness we must surrender ourselves to be consumed and realigned by His Holy Spirit and agape love. These are the source, agent and essence of the King's soldiers' prowess, the secret of our power and the means of our success. Once we reach this point, we actually become potentially invincible in Christ, but sadly we often don't realize this, and can still be tricked into failure. Yes, we will suffer in these battles, and from time to time the wounds inflicted may be quite serious. There will be insults, and some will try to mock, berate and shame us, just like they did to our Lord Jesus in days of old. The battle is surely hot and the campaign intense. It is a battle of life and death, ultimately to the death. There are only two possible outcomes: life in Christ, or eternal death without Him. There is no place to sit on the fence or be neutral. To do nothing is to fail personally, and to fail our marriages, families, churches, communities, villages, cities and nations. The future for ourselves and others, and the world around us, is in jeopardy just the same as it was for our soldiers going off to World War II. Many of those young men left homes, families, friends, jobs and a good life, and went off bravely knowing they may not return. They realized that if they did not wage this war, their whole world was at risk, including those most precious ones they left back home. If we reflect on this WWII scenario for just a moment, there are many significant parallels with these present dark and perilous days.

But how will we know whether we are winning this seismic battle, against the insanity of evil? The answer is that the *genuine peace* which I have described here at length, will begin to slowly emerge. Firstly, in small fleeting impressions, feelings, glimpses and visions... and then in flashes of faith, hope and sanity... This will be followed slowly and pervasively by a settled peace from Heaven, which will come gently upon our righteous armies and campaigners all over the world. An increasing confidence of a positive outcome will begin to emerge in every heart, on every front and in every nation. Finally, the enemy will begin to retreat, being overcome, exhausted and vanquished by the sustained power and determination of the saints in Christ Jesus, both living and gone before. The Peace of Christ *Genuine peace* will then begin to emerge systemically and pervasively. First as a trickle, then a gurgling stream, becoming a mighty river and ultimately an all-consuming flood until the whole earth is filled with The Glory of The Lord as the waters cover the sea... Oh what a wonderful day that will be, what a Divine joy. King Jesus, firstly manifest through His righteous followers, who will set a glowing and cohesive example to the world at large, bringing Godly leadership, Divine love, peace and His government to all domains of society, and eventually in the fullness of time, the victorious return of the King himself, in all

His Glory. Then mortals in right standing with God will become immortal in a moment. In the twinkling of an eye earthly bodies will be translated into heavenly. Evil will be judged and burned up by the purity and Glory of God, and our world will be transformed into a new phase of glorious existence, akin to heaven as we know it today.

Let's all work tirelessly toward that day!!!

Chapter 12 - Conclusion

In conclusion the battle for *genuine peace*, as I've said, starts in our own lives and is an internal, multi-facetted battle of massive proportions. The mind is the main frontier, and it is there that this momentous battle is often won or lost, temporarily... sometimes permanently. And it goes without saying that the campaign for peace in the family, church, community, village, city, nation and internationally is extremely difficult to wage, let alone win, if the parties involved have not yet achieved a modicum of peace in their own hearts. I pray this book has in some way helped you to further understand the nature and importance of *genuine peace*, and perhaps given some clues toward how to aspire to and eventually achieve this wonderful objective. Firstly, in our own personal domains then ultimately in the various other spheres of influence in which we operate.

No matter where we are on the journey of life, the achievement of *genuine peace* is always potentially possible, and the outcome is always thoroughly satisfying, to the point where, had we known earlier, I am sure we would have made this one of the key goals of our life. Then having achieved this precious jewel for ourselves, we can, and indeed must, position ourselves to help make it available to others we meet on the way.

I wish to sincerely and deeply thank you for taking the time to read this treatise, and for your persistence in wading through to the end. This book for me has been most challenging to write, due to the depth and complexity of the topic, and the need to remain brief in order to keep the book to a reasonable size. It has been like downloading from heaven a section of Encyclopedia Britannica, in loosely related jigsaw-size pieces, and then seeking to record the information in some orderly fashion on the head of a pin. I pray the Lord will guide you in taking the cameo segments, summaries and various styles of information presentation which you have just read, and bringing them together in your mind and heart, in a way which is helpful to you personally, and to those with whom you live, labour, and love.

I pray God's very best blessings upon you and yours, and that His presence, favour, guidance, wisdom, love, joy, peace and hope, will always be with you, as you journey daily, on your own quest for *Genuine peace*.

And as 2 Thessalonians 3:16 promises: Now the Lord of peace Himself give you peace always by all means. The Lord be with you all.

And finally, I leave with you the wonderful priestly blessing expressed in the timeless words of the book of Numbers chapter six and verses twenty-four to twenty-six from The Holy Bible. They serve to reinforce our Heavenly Father's favour toward us and are also the model He has given us to use in the blessing of others.

Numbers 6:24 -26: The Lord bless thee, and keep thee, The Lord make His face shine upon thee and be gracious unto thee, The Lord lift up His countenance upon thee and give thee peace!

And may this eternal and powerful life changing blessing always be yours, wherever you go and whatever you do in life and in the service of King Jesus.

Thank You

THE END